ASPEN PUBLISHERS

Friedman's
Practice Series

Property

Edited by

Professor Joel Wm. Friedman

Tulane University Law School
Jack M. Gordon Professor of Procedural Law & Jurisdiction

Wolters Kluwer

Law & Business

AUSTIN   BOSTON   CHICAGO   NEW YORK   THE NETHERLANDS

Aspen Publishers
Attn: Permissions Department
76 Ninth Avenue, 7th Floor
New York, NY   10011-5201

To contact Customer Care, e-mail customer.care@aspenpublishers.com,
call 1-800-234-1660, fax 1-800-901-9075, or mail correspondence to:

Aspen Publishers
Attn: Order Department
PO Box 990
Frederick, MD 21705

Printed in the United States of America.

1 2 3 4 5 6 7 8 9 0

ISBN 978-0-7355-7351-2

About Wolters Kluwer Law & Business

Wolters Kluwer Law & Business is a leading provider of research information and workflow solutions in key specialty areas. The strengths of the individual brands of Aspen Publishers, CCH, Kluwer Law International and Loislaw are aligned within Wolters Kluwer Law & Business to provide comprehensive, in-depth solutions and expert-authored content for the legal, professional and education markets.

CCH was founded in 1913 and has served more than four generations of business professionals and their clients. The CCH products in the Wolters Kluwer Law & Business group are highly regarded electronic and print resources for legal, securities, antitrust and trade regulation, government contracting, banking, pension, payroll, employment and labor, and healthcare reimbursement and compliance professionals.

Aspen Publishers is a leading information provider for attorneys, business professionals and law students. Written by preeminent authorities, Aspen products offer analytical and practical information in a range of specialty practice areas from securities law and intellectual property to mergers and acquisitions and pension/benefits. Aspen's trusted legal education resources provide professors and students with high-quality, up-to-date and effective resources for successful instruction and study in all areas of the law.

Kluwer Law International supplies the global business community with comprehensive English-language international legal information. Legal practitioners, corporate counsel and business executives around the world rely on the Kluwer Law International journals, loose-leafs, books and electronic products for authoritative information in many areas of international legal practice.

Loislaw is a premier provider of digitized legal content to small law firm practitioners of various specializations. Loislaw provides attorneys with the ability to quickly and efficiently find the necessary legal information they need, when and where they need it, by facilitating access to primary law as well as state-specific law, records, forms and treatises.

Wolters Kluwer Law & Business, a unit of Wolters Kluwer, is headquartered in New York and Riverwoods, Illinois. Wolters Kluwer is a leading multinational publisher and information services company.

CHECK OUT THESE OTHER GREAT TITLES:

Friedman's Practice Series
Outlining Is Important But PRACTICE MAKES PERFECT!

All Content Written By *Top Professors* • 100 Multiple Choice Questions • Comprehensive *Professor* Answers and Analysis for Multiple Choice Questions • *Real Law School* Essay Exams • Comprehensive *Professor* Answers for Essay Exams • Free Digital Version

Available titles in this series include:

Friedman's Civil Procedure

Friedman's Constitutional Law

Friedman's Contracts

Friedman's Criminal Law

Friedman's Criminal Procedure

Friedman's Property

Friedman's Torts

ASK FOR THEM AT YOUR LOCAL BOOKSTORE
IF UNAVAILABLE, PURCHASE ONLINE AT
HTTP://LAWSCHOOL.ASPENPUBLISHERS.COM

ABOUT THE EDITOR

Joel Wm. Friedman
Tulane Law School

Jack M. Gordon Professor of Procedural Law & Jurisdiction, Director of Technology

BS, 1972, Cornell University; JD, 1975, Yale University

Professor Joel Wm. Friedman, the Jack M. Gordon Professor of Procedural Law & Jurisdiction at Tulane Law School, is the lead author of two highly regarded casebooks -- "The Law of Civil Procedure: Cases and Materials" (published by Thomson/West) and "The Law of Employment Discrimination" (published by Foundation Press). His many law review articles have been published in, among others, the Cornell, Texas, Iowa, Tulane, Vanderbilt, and Washington & Lee Law Reviews.

Professor Friedman is an expert in computer assisted legal instruction who has lectured throughout the country on how law schools can integrate developing technologies into legal education. He is a past recipient of the Felix Frankfurter Teaching Award and the Sumpter Marks Award for Scholarly Achievement.

Table of Contents

PROPERTY
ESSAY EXAMS

QUESTIONS

PROPERTY ESSAY EXAM #1

Question # 1

The Federal Highway Beautification Act reads as follows:

> No billboard can be placed within 660 feet of interstate highways or other highways in which the United State government pays more than 50% of the cost of building such highways.

Public Interest Sign Company (hereafter PISC), a non-profit organization, purchases land adjacent to Exit 1000 of the I-80. PISC executes leases to the following organizations permitting them to erect billboards:

1. Borris Mart, PLC, a law firm specializing in personal injury cases. On his sign, he depicts an 18 wheeler crushing a mini-van with the words 'Check with me before you take their check'. His 800 number also appears.

2. Citizens for the Fourth Amendment, a lobbying group that seeks to control police searches of cars on interstate highways. On the sign are the following words: 'Just say NO to searches. Stopped by the cops? Dial 800-321-7654 before you let'em search'.

3. Gentlemen's Emporium, a one-stop adult book and video outlet. On the sign are the following words: 'Another burger? Why not have a more satisfying break at Gentlemen's Emporium. Next Right.'

Each group applies to Highway Commission for an exemption from the act on the grounds that the act as applied to their organization violates constitutionally protected rights.   You are counsel for the Highway Commission.   Does the act as applied violate the constitutional rights of any or all of the parties above?

Question 2

Clifford Chump is a partner in the prestigious Washington, DC based law firm, Chump and Chump. He owns a penthouse condo in the Beergate Building, located in a ten-story building over looking Lafayette Park, right across from 'the big white house on Pennsylvania Avenue'. From his balcony, Chump has a wonderful view of the District including the President's modest abode. Two months ago, Chump was catching rays on his balcony when he noticed a gray-haired gentleman in a ten gallon hat exiting a Black Lincoln Continental in front of the White House.   Excited he waived.   Secret Service agents on the roof of the White House witnessed the scene, and drew their Uzis.   Four well armed Secret Service agents charged into Chump's building, smashed down the door, burst onto the balcony and apprehended Chump.   The miserable old codger was, of course, weaponless; and the embarrassed Secret Service agents and apologized to him for the intrusion, citing the war on terror.

Last week Chump received a letter from the Director of the Secret Service. The Director outlined his concern that important guests use the particular entrance in question to attend state dinners. He enclosed a schedule and demanded that no persons be present on the balcony two hours before and two hours all listed state dinners. Moreover, they demanded the right to have two armed Secret Service personnel present on the balcony ten times during the next year in which state dinners were scheduled.

Chump, grumpy old man that he is, dashed a letter back in which he refused to comply, arguing a deprivation of property without due process of law. He would have cited the particular amendment to the Constitution that he considered infringed upon had he recalled its number. Chump sent an interoffice memorandum to the "Takings" department for which you clerk. Write a memorandum considering whether the Director of the Secret Service's request should be regarded as a taking, and if so what might be regarded as "just compensation".

Question #3

Bernard Uchello owned a three-story house in San Francisco called Birdhouse. From his roof top patio he could see, while looking north, the Golden Gate Bridge to his left and Coit Tower to his right. Many an evening he passed sipping Chardonnay watching the fog settle in. In 1995, Bernard retired from his tenured position at the Coit Tower School of Law. He could no longer afford such lavish accommodation on his meager pension and decided to divide his house into two separate dwellings. He would live in the west half, the Golden Gate side, and he would sell the east half, the Coit Tower side, to some yuppy lawyer with money to burn. Bernard found his mark, and sold the right half, now called East Birdhouse to Morrison Foerster, a wealthy new partner at the law firm of Dewey, Cheatem and Howe (my apologies to Car Talk fans). In order to secure his view he inserted the following clause:

> Clause 2,010.12 Vendee covenants for himself, his successors and assigns, not to build on the premises which in anyway obstructs the view of the west half of the house once known as Birdhouse.

Bernard and Morrison live happily as neighbors even sharing the occasional Cabernet. Alas the dot.com bust comes, and Morrison is sent packing in 2000. His current job with the City Attorney doesn't even reach six figures. In short he needs to sell his half of the Birdhouse. His broker finds a merchant banker, Alan Norris, who is still flush with cash, purchases East Birdhouse. The limitation above is not included in the deed from Foerster to Norris. When Norris receives his

2003 bonus, he decides to put a deck on his roof. Uchello sees the design and objects, because once built it will limit his view to only the top third of Coit Tower.

Bernard brings an action to enjoin the building of the deck in civil district court and for damages.

1. Should he prevail?

2. Suppose there was no Clause 1.010.12, is there another cause of action that Bernard might bring? How would that cause be resolved?

Question #4

Lisa Martin was a tenant in Pick-up Truck Apartments in Boot Cut on a year to year tenancy that commenced in August of 2001, and was automatically extended for a second year. The rent was $1,000 per month. On May 1st 2003, Lisa was lounging in her apartment watching her favorite video on MTV with her boy friend Nate, when shot gun pellets came streaming through the ceiling, and struck her in the leg, and Nate in the arm. The blast came from below, the apartment of Harry Ponoroff. Since he moved in February of 2003, Lisa's enjoyment of her apartment has been less than optimal. Harry threw wild parties on a regular basis, soirées that ended in the wee hours of the morning, and she could also hear violent fights below. When she informed the landlord, Richard Wall, of the problem, he told her that she ought to call the police. She did from time to time call the police, but the officers summoned told her to complain to her landlord. She did, and while Wall tried to talk to Harry about the situation, the problem continued.

Although the paramedics patched her wound and that of her beloved Nate, ugly scars remained. Shortly thereafter, without informing Wall, Lisa decided to move out of the premises, and on June 30th, both she and Nate filed individual actions in civil district court seeking damages in the amount of $500,000, consisting of medical bills, pain and suffering, and for the psychological trauma of having a scarred leg. In his answer, filed on July 31st, Wall denied liability for the injuries to both, and demanded $2,000 from Lisa, the rent for June and July. Moreover, he asked for a declaratory judgment that the lease extended to July 2004.

Consider the following questions:

1. Is the landlord liable for damages as alleged?

2. Is Lisa liable for the rent for June and July?

3. Was the lease extended, and for how long?

PROPERTY ESSAY EXAM #2

Question #1

Barry "Home Run King" Bonfield hit his 71st home run last night at Boot Cut Park in New Orleans, a major league record. The fat pitch was served up by Ralph "Number 13" Collins, star left-hander of the opposing team, the Slidell Yankees. Bonfield hit the homer into the bleachers where three Twolane Law faculty members were sitting swilling beer and hoping to catch a ball. The ball descended directly into the glove of Harry "Butterfingers" Ponoroff, but he (of course) bobbled the damn thing (caught it and then allowed it to fall out of said glove). It made its way into the lap of that eminent Sports Lawyer Cary Roberts, who had just dozed off. Sitting next to him was Ari Vice Griffin who picked the ball out of the Cary's lap, and left the park smiling.

Bonfield brought an action against Griffin in replevin (a common law form of action demanding the return of personal property wrongfully taken) in the District Court seeking the return of the ball, which, needless to say, is worth a pile. Ponoroff and Roberts intervened in the suit, each also demanding custody of the ball. And hang on, I believe I see Collins on his way to the courthouse, writ in hand. Not far behind him is Scott Coward, the owner of the Boot Cut Dwarfs, Bonfield's team, and also William Jefferson Clinton, the recently appointed Commissioner of Major League Baseball.

The case comes before Judge Hovenkurzt for whom you clerk. Baffled (as he always is), he asks you to write a memo considering the claims of each of the six parties. Recall that recently he read the comic book version of Locke's Two Treatises on Government, so don't forget to consider the so called 'labor theory of property' in your analysis.

Question #2

Ten years ago, Lox Cable Company purchased a right of way from George W. Lush to run wires across his Ranch in Crawford, Texas. The agreement was written as follows:

> For valuable consideration, the sum of $1000,000, the party of the first part, George W. Lush hereinafter referred to as W covenants and agrees with the party of the second part hereinafter referred to as Lox Cable that W shall permit the said Lox to erect pylons across the south forty acres of the land known as the Ranch at Crawford which the said Lush covenants that he owns in fee simple. Said pylons shall be placed at a distance of no more than twenty yards from each other. W further covenants and agrees to allow Lox to mount utility wires on the said pylons for the operation of cable television, and to allow Lox to maintain the said pylons and wires. This covenant shall bind successors.

Immediately thereafter, Lox Cable installed both the pylons and the wires, but unfortunately their lead engineer, the European trained Nigel Banks, placed the pylons twenty meters apart (a meter is about 39 inches rather than 36 inches). Lox operated the cable system in Crawford for 8 years. Two years Bagel Internet purchased ago Lox. In addition to offering cable services to customers, Bagel also provides what is known in the trade as 'high speed internet access' and local telephone service. In order to improve its 'connectivity', Bagel secured the services of Cappuccino Enterprises that installed a much larger fiber optic cable on the same pylons, but without removing the more modest cable installed by Lox. Bagel longer uses the Lox installed wire.

Once a month, Cappuccino sends an employee around to inspect the wires and pylons. In fact last month a severe tornado decimated a couple of pylons, and Cappuccino replaced them.

Shortly after the installation of the fifer optic cable, W's cattle grazing in the vicinity of the pylons became ill. W also discovered that the new cable generated a loud hum that disturbed him while he was watching his favorite programs on the Cartoon Network in his house that was about 15 yards from one of the pylons.

W brought an action in Crawford District Court seeking the following relief:

1. That Bagel's use of their interest in his property be enjoined on the grounds that it constitutes a nuisance both at common law, and under the Restatement (Second) of Torts (1977) sec. 822. Alternatively, W seeks damages in the sum of $50,000 per year for the next 20 years for lost profits from his cattle raising business and $25,000 for damage to his property.

2. That Bagel's use of their easement be enjoined and its use terminated on the grounds that the current use of the easement was inconsistent with the terms of the agreement. Alternatively, W seeks damages in the amounts set above in section 1.

3. That Bagel pay $30,000 for trespasses occasioned by their maintenance of the fiber optic wire and pylons.

So what do you think? Does W have a cause of action in nuisance or an action to terminate the easement? Argue both sides, offering competing considerations and arguments. Then assume that he does, which remedies would be a court be likely to grant.

Question #3

In 1882, Roundhead, the mayor and leading citizen of Boot Cut, conveyed one of her three mansions called Roachacre to the Cromwell Railway for $50,000. The deed contained the following limitation:

> To the Cromwell Railway and its heirs and assigns forever, but this interest shall cease if the Railway does not maintain rail passenger service to Boot Cut. At that time the land shall become a public park.

In 1959, the Railway sold Roachacre to Lisa Bologna for $500,000. Lisa renovated the mansion and transformed it into a high-end Italian Restaurant, a venue sadly needed in Boot Cut, called Le Catanese. Two years later, the Cromwell Railway merged with Abrosden Railway and ceased passenger service to Boot Cut, though it hired Jazepea Bus Line to transport prospective passengers to their terminal in Bunkie, 40 miles away. Alas demand was slack, and in May 2000, the service was discontinued.

It is now 2003. Le Catanese is so successful that Lisa appears regularly on the Food Channel, often as a guest of Emeril Legasse. She decides to abjure the kitchen entirely and move to Hollywood, and wants to sell the restaurant to her friend Juanita, who is convinced that Honduran food is the next craze that will hit Boot Cut connoisseurs. When Juanita's lawyer searches the title, she informs her that it is possible that Lisa does not have good title.

Lisa brings an action to quiet title in Boot Cut District Court, Judge Honor Off (for whom you clerk) presiding. Write a memo advising the learned judge should decide the case.

Question #4

In May of 1995, Alan Norris purchased a building in San Francisco called Bank's Dreamhouse, a fifteen story, low budget hotel. Fancying himself as a west coast Donald Trump, Norris's plan was to knock the dump down, and construct immediately a ten-story luxury apartment building called Buckingham Gate London Gardens on the lot. At the time of purchase there were no restrictions on building height in the area other than the following:

> San Francisco Municipal Code sec 19,765,789: All buildings primarily used for residential purposes in excess of ten stories constructed after 1990 must be erected according to standards published in Earthquake Regulation 16,345,675.

The following September, Norris hired Anne Bennatti, a world-renowned architect, to design Buckingham Gate London Gardens for $1,000,000. When he submitted her design for Buckingham Gate London Gardens, with projected building costs of $50,000,000, to the Building Inspector for approval on January 2, 1996, he was informed that there was a moratorium on building all buildings over five stories until earthquake ordinances were updated. Although he made frequent inquiries, it was not until January 2, 2000 that the City Council acted amending the above code section to include buildings over five stories in height. Bennatti's design did not conform to Earthquake Regulation 16,345,675. Norris sought a variance from the ordinance, and it was denied. Undaunted he reapplied for the permit, and again came up short. Reluctantly, he paid Bennatti an additional $1,000,000 to redraft the design according to Earthquake Regulation 16,345,675. The new cost of the building was $60,000,000, the additional $10,000,000 due to inflation in the construction trade as well as the additional costs of making the building conform to Earthquake Regulation 16,345,675.

Norris submitted the revised plans; they were approved and construction was completed last year. However, Norris decides to bring an action in District Court in San Francisco against the City alleging that the revised regulation constitutes a taking, and he seeks from the city the following damages:

(1) The additional cool million forked over to Anne Bennatti for the second set of plans.

(2) The additional cool ten million forked over to build a building that would comply with Earthquake Regulation 16,345,675.

(3) The sum of $2,546,768, which represents rental profits forgone for five years, which he calculates is a loss attributable to the City for failure to issue a building permit on January 2, 1996.

Can he prevail on any or all of his claims?

PROPERTY ESSAY EXAM #3

Question #1

In 2099, the Twolane Law School published a directory of it illustrious alumni. It was able to do so because the Assistant Vice Director of Alumni Affairs' assistant spent the entire summer scouring through the Law School records to ascertain the names of graduates, and then compiled an accurate list of their present whereabouts by "googling" each name. The purpose of the exercise was to enable the Assistant Vice Director of Development to contact said alums in order to put the bite on them for a donation to the Weinmann Hall building enlargement project. In addition, the information was printed and bound in green leather (well maybe it was plastic), and offered for sale at $100, enabling the Law School to make an immediate profit of $75 from each book. Wiley old Professor Bonfield, now retired, springs for the $100, scans it, reprints it, and offers for sale a leather-bound version on his web site **ripoffs.com** for $75, content to make a more modest profit.

The Board of Trustees of Twolane University sue to enjoin the sale of Bonfield's version of the Alumni volume and for damages in the amount of $75 for each book Prof B. has sold. The case comes before Judge Hovenkurtz for whom you clerk. Should they prevail? In writing your answer, address the following:

1. What principles of intellectual property law can be applied to this case?

2. Can concepts derived from the law of finders and capture be applied to the case?

Question # 2

In late 1965, Zonoroff Inc, a mining company, opened its Toolane silver mine in the hills over-looking the City of Boot Cut. In order to reach most easily the new mine from the main highway into Boot Cut, the I-70118, Harry, chief engineer, cut a road through the grass land of Crawford Ranch, a spread of impressive size owned by Giuseppe Waldegrave Cespuglio (hereafter G. W.) in early spring 1965. The following year, Gary, Zonoroff's chief communications specialist, ran a telephone wire on poles erected through Crawford Ranch, slightly to the left of the newly cut road. Both activities were largely unknown to its owner G. W. who was at Zale University, back east studying International Relations and having 'a ole good time', not necessarily in that order.

In 1992, after receiving his A. A. degree, cum laude, and suffering an unsuccessful try at national political office, G. W. returned to Boot Cut to take up ranching. In Aggie Management 101, G. W. learned (he took the course three times) that the first step a successful rancher must undertake is to fence in his spread. This he did. But when Barry, chief maintenance man of Zonoroff Inc., saw the fence he objected because it blocked the road cut by Harry. G. W. removed the part of the fence that blocked the right of way cut by Harry, and installed locked gates at either end. He delivered a key to Cary, chief property manager of Zonoroff Inc., saying that the company could use the right of way 'with his permission'. Always the good neighbor, Zonoroff Inc. decided to use the more circuitous route to Boot Cut, but Cary kept the key.

It is now 2004. As you may know the price of silver has recently gone sky high. In order to service the mine, Ari, chief mining engineer at Zonoroff Inc., decides to increase operations. In order to do so, he brings in large earthmovers that fill a continuous stream of dump trucks that use the road through Crawford Ranch. Because silver mining has gone high tech, Ari also has fiber optic cables installed on the telephone poles as well as high - tension electrical wires. The extensive use of the road makes it more difficult for G. W. to use the road for his feed lot operation, and the heavy loads carried by the dump trucks start to generate potholes. G. W. decides to move the operation clear on the other side of his spread. To do so, he closes down the operation for two months, incurring lost profits in the amount of $20,000, relocation expenses amounting to $10,000, and $100,000 in damages incurred because of additional monthly costs of using the new feed lot over its useful life.

In 2004, Zonoroff Inc. brings an action in civil district court to enjoin G. W. from blocking the road cut in 1965. In addition, Zonoroff seeks an order allowing it to maintain the right of way and charge the expense to G. W. G. W. resists both the injunction and the order for maintenance of the road. He demands in a counterclaim that Zonoroff Inc. remove all wires and poles from his spread. Alternatively, he claims that the use of the road by Zonoroff Inc. is a nuisance. He seeks to enjoin the use of the road as such, and damages in the amount of $130,000 for the telephone wires. Write a memo addressing the issues as follows:

1. Was an easement to use the road cut by Harry created? If so, when, and how?

2. What was the legal effect of placing the gate and changing the locks?

3. If the court orders continued use of the road and Zonoroff repairs the road, can Zonoroff recoup those expenses from G. W.?

4. Should Zonoroff Inc. be ordered to remove the poles and wires?

5. Should an injunction be issued restraining further use of the road by Zonoroff Inc. as a nuisance, and should damages of $130,000 be ordered?

Question #3

In order to stem the erosion of the banks of the Boot Cut River, the Army Corps of Engineers added in 2001 sheet steel piling to jetties on its own property. The pilings direct water downstream, and away from the river's critical fork with Toolane Creek. The result of the diversion, however, is to cause greater erosion to downstream owners, in particular, Alan Norris. The Army Corps over the last three years has attempted as part of its mitigation program to deposit land and rocks on the shoreline. Despite these efforts, the river has absorbed over three yards of his riparian land. Previously, Norris used the land submerged by the diverted river water as a campground and tubing spot, yielding $50,000 per year in profit. The Army Corp projects that the water will recede over the next ten years, and the land in question will no longer be submerged. In fact, the land will eventually extend three feet into the river, enlarging the extent of Norris's property. According to experts consulted by Norris, however, it is not clear when, if ever, the land submerged will once again be dry land.

After exhausting all administrative remedies, Norris brings an action in Federal District Court arguing a taking.

1. Consider whether, given current law, a taking has occurred.

2. Assume that a taking has occurred; assess 'just compensation'.

PROPERTY ESSAY EXAM #4

Question # 1

Archangelo Duebomber (hereinafter Due), a survivalist, has camped on Boot Cut Stream in a remote section of Shermanfork Ranch in Texas since last April (1999). As winter set in, Due decided to make his temporary accommodation weatherproof by building a cabin. As luck would have it, he spied a dozen white pine logs tied together with a rope floating down Boot Cut Stream. He hauled them out of the stream, and worked them with his primitive tools into a comfortable cabin.

After spending the harsh winter in isolation, Due decided to return to civilization and attend law school. In June (2000), short of cash, he approached Ned Shermanfork the owner of Shermanfork Ranch, and asked him if he would like to purchase the cabin from him. Ned declined, and ordered Due "off my spread". Enraged at his ungentlemanly conduct, Due blasted Shermanfork with the survivalist weapon of choice, the AZ 47000. Fortunately, he only inflicted what is commonly called (in Texas) a flesh wound. The story made the morning edition of the Boot Cut Times. Scott Coward, the leasee of Shermanfork's prime timberland, read the story, and emailed Shermanfork indicating to him that the logs must have been cut by his men who were at the time (during the fall) culling the forest and floating the proceeds down the Boot Cut River. According to Coward, the logs must have broken loose and floated into Boot Cut Stream. He demanded the return of the white pine logs or their value. Shermanfork refused.

Due brings an action in Boot Cut District Court demanding from Shermanfork the value of the cabin, or alternatively, return of the dozen white pine logs or their value. Coward intervenes demanding the cabin, the return of the white pine logs or their value.

You clerk for Judge Wig. She asks you to write a brief memorandum assessing the basis for each of the three individual claims to the cabin and/or the white pine logs.

Question #2

Since 1985, Richard Wall has operated a modest rooming house in the Bowery section of Swamp populated by low income individuals. The premises, fondly known as Wall's Flophouse, consisted of a dozen one room habitations. Last month the building was severely damaged by a fire. Reconstruction would cost $5,000,000; Wall is reluctant to make such investment, given that the Flophouse generated a profit last year of only $50,000. Wall pondered demolishing the structure, and he employed an architect to design a multi-plex cinema for the lot; price tag $10,000,000, projected yield $250,000. Last month, Wall applied to the city of Swamp for a permit to build a cinema.

The city of Swamp denied the permit citing the Provision of Low Income Housing Act of 1994 which provides as follows:

> Section 2,345,678   No owner or lessee of property that is devoted to the housing low income persons may demolished the property:
>
> (a)   the property has been destroyed and it is infeasible to repair, or,
>
> (b)   the owner or lessee has agreed to build and operate a similar number of units elsewhere in the city of Swamp.
>
> (c)   the owner or lessee establishes extreme hardship for an exemption from this section.

Wall brings an action in District Court alleging that the ordinance is 'taking'. He seeks either a court order directing the city to issue a permit, or alternatively, that the city pay damages of $10,000,000, the present value of his anticipated profits for the next twenty years.

The case comes before Judge Gown for whom you clerk. She asks you to produce a memo considering whether the Provision of Low Income Housing Act is an unconstitutional taking, and, if she should so rule, what measure of compensation she should order.

Question #3

In July of 1999, Jasepea Mazeratti signed a five-year lease as a tenant in the Blissful Ignorance Shopping Centre located in North Swamp. The form lease contained the following clause: "The demised premises shall be used for commercial purposes only".

On the said leasehold premises, Jasepea runs a fashionable Italian restaurant called the "Il Spaghetteria". Times are tough: spaghetti is out; in order to save on expenses, Jasepea moved his personal belongings, and a fold-out sofa bed, into his small office behind the kitchen in mid-January.

This winter has been particularly severe in Swamp. Ice and snow removal at the Shopping Centre has been spotty at best. Last month, Jasepea had to phone five times before the snowplows cleared parking spots in front of his door. When he asked the maintenance person to sprinkle de-icing pellets on the walkway in front of his restaurant daily, he stacked five bags in front of his door with the following written on the top bag: "Do it yourself; it ain't my job". Yesterday, Jasepea's lone customer, Beatrice Wall, slipped and fell at the entrance to the restaurant. Even though Jasepea ripped up the check, she has threatened to sue.

Jazepea has decided he wants out of the spaghetti business. He put on his snowshoes, and walked across the car park to your office. He says to you: "I can't make a go of this business. I'm moving back to Sacramento. Can I get out of this lease? How? And can Beatrice sue me? If she does can I sue the [expletive deleted] landlord for reimbursement?"

In return for representation, Jasepea promises you pasta for life. Answer his questions.

Question #4

In 1990, Alan Norris purchased a house (36 Ambrosden Avenue) in a subdivision called Ashley Gardens. A person of modest income, Norris purchased property at the bottom of a very steep hill. Shortly after his purchase, Norris's house was overrun by a series of mudslides from the top of the hill, to the west of his property. To protect his house from what he regarded as his neighbor's mud, Norris contracted with an architect to build a stone-restraining wall on the west boundary line. In order to secure further the wall from frequent mudslides, the architect attached multi-colored concrete beams to the side of Norris's house that was about five feet from the property line. Norris also negotiated with his next-door neighbor (34 Ambrosden Avenue) Sal Benanatti, for the right to build a ditch on the other side of the wall (on Sal's land) in order to divert water away from the wall. A written agreement was entered into with the following terms:

> For value received, Sal Benanatti and his heirs and assigns, party of the first part, agree to maintain a drainage ditch on property known as 34 Ambrosden Avenue, in Ashley Gardens, which shall be constructed by Alan Norris, party of the second part. Said agreement shall be recorded in the Ashley Gardens Record Office.

The agreement was duly recorded, but shortly thereafter a drought began; Sal never maintained the ditch.

Last year Sal retired to Florida, and sold 34 Ambrosden Avenue to Jesse Ventura. Jesse indicated to Norris that he found the concrete beams an eyesore, and asked him to dismantle them citing the following clause (2,345,678) in all the deeds to houses in Ashley Garden:

> With the exception of stone walls no property owner may build within five feet of his or her property line.

Norris refuses, and Jesse brings an action in nuisance or alternatively to enforce clause 2,345,678 seeking the removal of the concrete beams.

In the course of the litigation, Jesse discovers that the wall built by Norris is actually two feet over the property line, and amends his complaint to seek its removal. He also refuses to maintain the ditch, and after torrential rains water begins to run on to the Norris's property. Norris amends his complaint seeking an injunction ordering Jesse to maintain the ditch, and seeking to quite title to the lad up to the stone wall.

The case comes before Judge Wig and Gown for whom you clerk. She asks you to consider each of Jesse's claims, and each of Norris's claims.

Assume the following statute is in force in Ashley Gardens:

> No person may bring an action for the recovery or possession of a property interest unless that person commences an action or makes an entry within five years after the right to commence an action or make an entry first accrued.

PROPERTY ESSAY EXAM #5

Question #1

After working ten long years at the Twolane Law School, Professor Carmellow Youchello finally earned a sabbatical. Never one to appreciate the southern climes, Youchello decided to spend the fall in the splendid isolation of southern Maine. He rented a mansion on a private island owned by a former Twolane Dean Jack Bob Remark. One day, while snooping around the attic, Youchello uncovered a musty old volume of Sir Henry Maine's <u>Ancient Law</u>. On the reverse side of the dust jacket, he discovered scattered notes entitled "Plot for a Movie". Youchello read the scribbles, jotted down notes, and called his old college roommate Stephen Spielberg. Spielberg loved it; something about a cute little extra-terrestrial that finds happiness in America, and a star is born. Youchellow collects $1,000,000 in royalties, and buys a vineyard in Tuscany.

Two years later, ex-Dean Remark uncovered the Maine volume while browsing through his collection in Maine. As luck would have it, he noticed the scribbles. A movie aficionado, Remark immediately recognized the plot as that of ET. He confronted Spielberg, who confronted Youchellow who, as usual, shrugged his shoulders.

Remark brings an action in District Court against Youchello and Spielberg for $50,000,000, the profits made on the movie. News of the lawsuit is plastered all over the "media", and Richard Wall learns of the action. Wall intervenes in the suit claiming that he owned the book, and sold it to Remark; he seeks $50,000,000 in damages.

The case with the full cast of characters comes before Judge Honor Off for whom you clerk. He asks you to evaluate the legal basis for the claims of each party, and as always, he is relying upon you to guide him as to which claim is the strongest.

Question #2

Jasepea Maseratti owns a small home on a quarter acre lot in Palookaville in a sub-division called Roundhead Estates. He purchased the house from Valerio Luciano, who bought the palatial dwelling from the developer, Lisa Martin. The sub-division was advertised a "High Class Residential Community." In the plat filed in the County Registry Office no use limitations were noted. In the deed from Martin Associates to Luciano was the following clause:

Restrictions:

For use as a single-family dwelling.

Uses that diminish the residential character of the premises are prohibited.

When the property was sold to Maseratti no clause of restriction similar to the above was included.

Maseratti decided to build a replica of the Leaning Tower of Pisa in his front yard. He hired an architect to design an edifice to 1/10 scale or about 25 yards high. A permit was issued, and building commenced.

The neighbors are not happy. They banded together and asked the City Council to pass a zoning ordinance that prohibits the building of such a folly. An ordinance was proposed with the following provision:

Towers, leaning or otherwise, may not be built on residential land in Roundhead Estates.

By the time the ordinance was adopted, Maseratti's tower was nearly complete. The City Council brought an action to enjoin further construction on the grounds that the building contemplated violates the ordinance. In addition, the City Council raised the deed restriction mentioned above, and sought to enjoin further construction on the grounds that the building is large enough to accommodate another family and is an eyesore.

Maseratti counterclaims seeking to enjoin the enforcement on the ordinance on the ground that it constitutes a "taking". Alternatively, if the court enforces the ordinance, he asks for compensation in the amount of $100,000 (the building costs thus far expended plus the cost to tear the tower down), with an additional $100,000 "loss of property value.

Because the case raises so many important issues at such a high level of abstraction, the case is referred to Judge Honor Off. He asks you to write a memorandum discussing the strengths and weaknesses of the City Council's position, as well as the Maserrati counterclaim. Should he find that ordinance is a taking, he wonder what would be just compensation.

Question #3

Alan Norris owns a modest shotgun house in the State of Swamp. Due to the high cost of draining land and building in Swamp, houses are rather close together. Security is a problem in Swamp, and the Stouts (who have lived in the adjacent house for the past twenty years) have decided to attach a spotlight to their house to illuminate the alleyway between the two houses (Norris/Stout). Unfortunately, in order for the spotlight to illuminate the alleyway, light must shine through the french doors at the rear of the Norris' sun porch. The precise spot where the light shines in is an awkward one, because Norris has installed a golden aviary for his two rare species pet canaries right at the point of greatest illumination. The glare of the spotlight keeps the canaries awake at night (and their singing does the same for Norris). This year the canaries have failed to breed: each chick is worth $500. Although Norris has explained the situation to the Stouts, they refuse to redirect their spotlight.

(1) A groggy Alan Norris comes into your office and asks you if there is some remedy. Don't suggest sleeping pills – it is a LAW office.

(2) Assume the situation has been ongoing since May 1, 1989, and the following statute is in force:

> No person may bring an action for recovery or possession of real property unless the person who makes a claim of right has commenced an action for recovery of the real property no longer than ten years after the claim of right has accrued.

What would your advice be?

Question #4

Ed Sherman loves coffee. It has been his dream to open a coffee shop in the vicinity of the Law School, and spend his infrequent idle moments dispensing coffee and ruminating on the latest advances in mediation procedures with inquiring young minds. Next door to the Law School is a small house used by the University to accommodate the Vice Dean. Because the Law Faculty voted to terminate the office, it became available for rent. Sherman negotiated a five-year lease with the University commencing on January 1, 1998 with the following provision:

> "Tenant agrees to use the premises only for the sale of coffee, tea and bagels only."

Sherman's business prospered, but in the following year, Buckstar, a national chain, opened a larger, more attractive facility around the corner, selling coffee and a variety of other drinks, as well as, exotic pastries. Profits at Sherman's coffee shop plunged. To make matters worse for poor Sherman, a link has been recently discovered between eating bagels (which account for 94.5% of Sherman's profit) and various diseases including cancer. Demand for bagels has plunged, and Sherman's business has fallen into the red. In order to improve his profit picture, Sherman began to sell croissants, and has proposed to tutor law students on the side.

University's president decides that the altered complexion of Sherman's business is not conducive to the collegiate atmosphere on Ferret Street. University notifies Sherman that Campus Security will begin to intercept trucks that deliver croissants, and should Sherman continue to provide nourishment other than in the round form with holes (and donuts don't count) University will seek to terminate the lease on the grounds that Sherman is in breach of a material provision thereof. Sherman refuses to yield, and University commences an action to terminate the lease, seeking damages in the amount of $5,000, the rental payments due under the remaining term. Sherman counterclaims seeking, in the alternative, either rescission of the lease or an order enjoining University from interfering with the delivery of croissants. In either case, Sherman also petitions for the value of the lease and for lost profits.

The case comes before Judge Honor Off for whom you clerk. Prepare a memorandum considering the following questions:

1.   Should Tulane be able to terminate the lease and seek the rent for the entire term on the grounds that Sherman has violated an express term of the lease by selling croissants and offering tutoring?

2.   Should Sherman be able to enjoin Tulane's croissant blockade, or alternatively, rescind the lease?

PROPERTY
ESSAY EXAMS

ANSWERS

PROPERTY ESSAY EXAM #1

Question #1

I.   Mart v. Commission

1.   Exercise of police powers

The FHBA is a zoning law, and as such must be justified under the police power, the government's right to limit land use in order to protect the public from harm. Both state and federal courts have found that environmental regulation is with the ambit of the police power. Though dealing with amenities, the act is a valid exercise of the police power.

2.   Fifth Amendment taking

Though a valid exercise of the police power, a zoning law may clash with constitutional rights, and therefore be invalid as applied to individual conduct. Borris Mart will argue that the ordinance as applied to him is a taking of his property (his lease of the sign) which will require just compensation under the Fifth Amendment. Should he receive just compensation for the loss of his sign and perhaps lost profits from accident victims, the court will deny his claim. A property owner will receive compensation only when his primary expectations are thwarted. When Bart leased the sign he should have known of the law. He assumed the risk of its enforcement.

3.   First Amendment

Borris Mart will argue that enforcement of the ordinance should be enjoined because it violates his First Amendment right to free speech the ordinance as applied to him. The court should find that his speech is commercial rather than political, and in such cases the legislature need only show that there is a rational basis for their exercise of the police power that, there is connection between signs and accidents, and/or signs despoil the environment.

II.   Citizens v. Commission

1.   Exercise of police powers

The FHBA is a zoning law, and as such must be justified under the police power, the government's right to limit land use in order to protect the public from harm. Both state and federal courts have found that environmental regulation is with the ambit of the police power. Though dealing with amenities, the act is a valid exercise of the police power.

2.   First Amendment

Though a valid exercise of the police power, a zoning law may clash with constitutional rights, and therefore be invalid as applied to individual conduct. Citizens for the Fourth Amendment have a strong claim to enjoin the enforcement of the FHBA as applied to them. They are exercising their free speech rights, and are also assisting others in protecting their Fourth Amendment rights. Moreover, their speech is directly linked to the conduct in question. Don't let them violate your rights here. The free speech claim triggers strict scrutiny, and the court will have to decide whether the ban is absolutely necessary to protect the environment, and whether such environmental legislation is critical. The state may claim that there are other ways of getting the message across, such as leaflets in rest stops or radio spots. If the balance turns in favor of the law's validity, the same just compensation argument obtains.

III.   Gentlemen's Emporium

1.   Exercise of police powers

The FHBA is a zoning law, and as such must be justified under the police power, the government's right to limit land use in order to protect the public from harm. Both state and federal courts have found that environmental regulation is with the ambit of the police power. Though dealing with amenities, the act is a valid exercise of the police power.

2.   First Amendment

Although a valid exercise of the police power, a zoning law may clash with constitutional rights, and therefore be invalid as applied to individual conduct. Gentleman's Emporium is also exercising commercial speech. However, they may argue that their advertising is linked to free expression, erotic dancing. Were the court to concede the link, scrutiny would be of the intermediate variety. The court would require the state to demonstrate that it was not trying indirectly to regulate the conduct by banning the advertisement. Likewise, if other advertising modes are available, it would be possible inform travelers of the protected conduct.

Question #2

I.   Chump v. Secret Service

1.   Fifth Amendment taking

When government conduct requires a property owner to suffer a trespass, a fundamental stick in the bundle of property owner's rights, the right to exclude, has been abrogated. However, not all trespasses give rise to a 'taking' requiring just compensation under the Fifth Amendment. Takings jurisprudence has focused upon two factors: 1. the character of the trespass; and 2. its economic impact. As to character, the court always finds a taking when government requires permanent physical occupation. Chump will argue that although the Secret Service will not always be on his property, he cannot control the time, place and manner of the physical occupation, rendering it tantamount to a permanent presence. That is stretch, and the court will probably regard the occupation as temporary. Chump will argue that the economic impact of the trespass is great; that his privacy is invaded at various times, and that the value of the property to him is substantially impaired. While the calendar is planned in advance, he will argue that his activities must be planned to coincide with the Secret Service's demands. He will also argue that a buyer who knew of the ongoing trespasses would be reluctant to pay the full market value of similar property situated elsewhere.

2.   Just compensation

When property is taken, the government must pay just compensation. The measure of just compensation is what a willing buyer would pay a willing seller for the property taken. The calculation is difficult to make in this case. Chump will argue that the Secret Service is a tenant, and they should pay rent for the period of occupation. Moreover, each day they move in, he is required in some sense to move out. He would calculate the rental value of his penthouse per day, add to it the cost of alternative accommodation, and the expense of relocation, and suggest that such is the proper measure of damages. The Secret Service will argue that they have merely acquired occupation for a couple of hours, and that takings law does not require compensation for losses suffered by landowners, only value that has been acquired. They would argue that a realtor should calculate the difference between the fair market value without the intrusion and the fair market value with it. That amount would be likely be minimal, particularly since the emergency may not be ongoing. Their calculation will be accepted.

Question # 3-1

I.   Bernard v. Norris

1.   Covenant running with the land

For Bernard to prevail requires that the promise in Clause 2,010.12 run with the land. Norris will argue that the promise was not included in his deed, and even if it was Bernard was not a party to the transfer.   However, Bernard will claim successfully that the promise in the deed from him to Foerster runs with the land.   Though jurisdictions differ in specifics, property law has established four requirements to allow a promisee to enforce a promise made by another to be enforced against a subsequent owner, to run with the land: intent to bind successors; horizontal privity; vertical privity, and touch and concern.

2.   Intent

The agreement specifies that successors should be bound evincing intent that the promise binds subsequent owners.

3.   Horizontal Privity

The promise was made between was a buyer and a seller. Although some jurisdictions require the parties to have mutual interests in each other's land, most jurisdictions find horizontal privity when an owner subdivides land.   This is the case here.   When the promise is created by those in horizontal privity it is more certain that subsequent owners know of the restriction since subdivision is one of the time points in the change of title that attracts the attention of title searches.

4.   Vertical Privity

Vertical privity exists because the promisee and the party against whom the promise is to be enforced were parties to a legal transfer: Foerster conveyed to Norris.

5.   Touch and Concern

Touch and concern has many different meanings, but the common thread is that the promise benefits the promisee's land. This it does. Initially, real covenants were enforced through damages; Norris could build, but was required to reimburse Bernard for the lost value of his land.

6.   Equitable Servitude

Regardless of whether the requirements of a real covenant were met, the agreement created an equitable servitude. To ask a court of equity to enjoin construction, Bernard need only prove intent to bind successors and notice. Both are present. The intent to bind successors is expressed; and vendees have notice of all provisions in their chain of title. Because Norris has yet to build, an injunction is a proper remedy.

II.   Bernard v. Foerster

1.   Breach of contract

Foerster promised Bernard that neither he nor his successors would obstruct B's view. While Bernard may sue Foerster for breach of contract, Bernard would really enjoin Norris from constructing the offending building. Moreover, it may not be practical to sue Foerster, who having moved, may be out of the jurisdiction, or may not be able to pay the requisite measure of damages.

Question #3-2

I.   Bernard v. Norris

1.   Equitable servitude
It is doubtful that an equitable servitude would have been created that would run with the land. Intent

and notice could only be proved by evidence of oral discussions. Although equitable servitudes need not be embodies in a transfer, they almost invariably are created by reference to a writing, even if the promise is absent from the deed.

Question #4-1

I. Lisa & Nate v. Wall

1. Landlord common law tort liability

Landlords are generally not liable for damages arising from torts suffered by tenants. The common law limited landlord tort liability to situations in which landlord knew of a defect and concealed it from the tenant, the landlord fixed some defect poorly, or the tort occurred in common areas. This is not the case in this situation. She knew about her neighbor's violent temperament, the landlord did not undertake steps to quell it, and the tort occurred in her apartment. However, Lisa will argue that landlord had a duty to protect her, and that obligation has been breached. Courts have been more willing to extend landlord liability when safety issue are in play, for example, where, for example, defective or inadequate locks have been provided. Lisa will argue that she informed the landlord, and he inadequately responded to her request, but absent an expressed promise to guard her safety, the claim is not actionable. Her remedy should be against the tortfeasor and not the landlord.

2. Constructive eviction

A tenant is absolved of obligations under a lease if the landlord's conduct amounts to a constructive eviction. So Lisa will argue that the dangerous situation amounted to a constructive eviction. Lisa must prove that the landlord had some obligation that landlord did not perform; that due to the omission the value of the premises to her was impaired; that the landlord had notice, and that after a reasonable time she vacated. While the landlord might not have been responsible to compensate under a tort theory, the landlord has made an implied warranty of quiet enjoyment. While that warranty generally applies to only landlord's own conduct, it may extend to an obligation that other tenants not disturb the peace. Lisa can demonstrate that the violent conduct was ongoing, and that the landlord had notice of the breach and failed to remedy it. She vacated on June 30th, so she should argue that she is responsible only for June's rent. The difficult point would be to persuade the court that it should extend the warranty to the conduct of landlord's other tenants.

Question #4-2

I.   Landord v. Lisa

    1.   Implied Warranty of Habitability

Lisa will argue that landlord breached the implied warranty of habitability. Landlords though statutes or through reform of the common law are held to an obligation to provide premises which are fit to live in. Lisa can argue that the danger and the bullet holes to boot render the premises uninhabitable. The amount of rent should reflect the difference between its fair market value as warranted and the fair market value as is. Breach would also allow her to quit. Thus she could claim back some rent paid, pay the diminished amount for June, and be absolved of her obligation for July. Her argument is fairly strong though the question of safety is a difficult one since it is questionable as to whether or not the premises were really uninhabitable.

Question #4-3

I.   Landlord v. Lisa

1.   Notice of termination

Lisa will argue that her vacation of the premises and commencement of suit was sufficient to give notice that she wished to terminate her year to year as of July 31st. Lisa had a year-to-year tenancy. The tenancy would continue for a further year unless either landlord or tenant gave notice that the tenancy should terminate. Notice is a formal legal statement. Conduct is insufficient. The lawsuit with its various claims, including constructive eviction, filed on the 30th is likely sufficient notice.

PROPERTY ESSAY EXAM #2

Question #1

I.   Bonfield v. Griffin

1.   Labor theory of property

Bonfield has a greater right to possession under the labor theory of property. Using Locke's theory Bonfield will argue that a major league baseball is worth about $10; the fact that this particular ball is far more valuable is due to his skill and perseverance. Its value has been increased by his labor. Griffin, on the other hand, is merely fortunate that the ball landed so close to him; his labor did not increase the value of the ball. Indeed none of the other claimants save Coward and Clinton have expended labor to increase the value of the ball. While they organized the sport, thousands of balls are knocked out of the park, and their value is far more modest than this record-breaking homer.

2.   Law of capture

Griffin will argue that he is the present possessor, and therefore under the law of capture or finders, his right is superior to all save the true owner. The true owner has abandoned the ball. Therefore his right is paramount. Under the law of capture he will argue that he deprived this wild ball (owned by nobody) of its natural liberty; neither Ponoroff nor Roberts were able to do so. Alternatively, he found the ball in Roberts lap. He was in the bleachers lawfully; it is a public place. Roberts never reduced the ball to his possession; therefore he cannot claim to have been the finder. Indeed he never knew the ball had landed on his lap. Likewise, Ponoroff never possessed the ball; he never caught it, which is presumably how baseballs are possessed.

Bonfield will claim that when he hit the ball, he had possession, and he never intended to abandon it. Again, the reasonable assumption is that balls out of play go to the fan that caught it. Either Bonfield never had possession, or he abandoned it.

II.   Collins v. Griffin

1.   Law of capture

Collins will argue that he was a possessor, and that by pitching the ball he never intended to abandon it. That won't do. Pitchers don't claim rights in the ball; nor do they expect to keep it when the ball they pitch is hit out of play. Either Collins never had possession, or he abandoned it.

Question #2

I.   W v. Bagel

1. Easement

The agreement created an easement in gross to erect pylons in specified fashion. When an interest in property is created, and not appurtenant to its holders land, it is personal and is to be held in gross. Here the easement is Lox's property not part of its ownership rights in land. Easements in gross rather like most property interests are transferable, absent express understanding to the contrary. Therefore when Bagel purchased Lox, it acquired the easement. That there was a technical error in installation should not be cause for termination of the easement. Unless the mistake was material, Bagel should continue to be able to use the easement. Depending on the jurisdictions statute of limitations period (less than 7 years), the pylon easement might have been created by prescription. The pylons were open and notorious, and continuously on the property. But if they were there as a product of mistake, the

requisite adversity might not be present. Bagel will argue that there was no permission manifested to place the pylons incorrectly, and therefore their conduct was adverse. Either argument will support Bagel's claim for an easement.
Nuisance

2. Nuisance

Assuming the easement is valid, the conduct of bagel may be a nuisance if W can prove that the gravity of the harm to him of Bagel's conduct outweighs its social utility. Unlike the common law, which generally followed the first in time doctrine (W there prior to Bagel, he may continue his conduct), the Restatement uses an economic balancing test. W would argue that the harm is considerable, lost profits from ranching, an activity to which the land is well suited. He would also argue that high speed internet in rural areas, in the age of wireless, is not as useful to the economy as ranching. Bagel will argue progress; that the social utility of ranching is not low, but is not as great as bringing new technology to rural areas. W would respond that if the utility is high, the true cost ought to be paid by Bagel's customers, rather than free riding on W's lost property value. W may argue the second Restatement formulation: that the conduct is a nuisance if it is serious and the actor can afford to continue the operation and pay compensation. This argument plays into the same theme as above: why cannot Bagel assume the costs of moving his operation, or compensate W for losses by passing the costs on to Bagel's customers. While W might pose the same question, it seems clear that the intentional invasion required by nuisance comes from Bagel's land use and not Ws.

3. Modernization

The installation of the larger wires is likely not inconsistent with the terms of the easement. Bagel will argue that it ought to be able to modernize the easement by placing a thicker wire. The agreement is silent about the wire, and specific about the pylons suggesting that the girth of the wire was not an essential element of the bargain. The wires are high tension, and W may argue that it was implicit in the agreement that the use of the easement would not affect his own use of land. Still lack of specificity requires the court to consider what was in the parties' reasonable contemplation. Here modernization seems reasonable given the enterprise.

4. Secondary easement

Inspections are also within the scope of the easement. Generally, the obligation to maintain the easement falls on the holder of the dominant interest: the party who reaps the benefit of the easement. Courts therefore permit the holder to enter on to servient land (the parcel subject to the easement) to maintain the easement. Here Bagel seeks only to exercise that right. The right to inspect and maintain (sometimes referred to as a secondary easement) is implied within the scope of the easement.

Question #3

I.   Lisa v. District Court

1.   Fee simple

The conveyance of 1882 created a fee simple subject to an executory interest. The conveyance to an individual or corporate entity 'and her/his/their heirs 'creates a fee simple absolute.

2.   Defeasable fee simple

This fee simple absolute has a limitation annexed; generally such limitations are unenforceable, except those that restrict uses. These are called deafeasable fee simples. Because the restriction is not on land use, the limitation cuts off the fee simple not when it ceases to use the land for railroad purposes, but when the rail road no longer serves Boot Cut, it is a fee simple absolute followed by an executory interest in the city, which would presumably have the obligation to maintain the property as a park. Lisa bought the land from the railroad while trains were operating, and had good title probably until the bus stopped running, the effective termination of rail service. Even though the interest in the city may not vest longer than a life in being plus 21 years, the interest is not subject to the rule against perpetuities, because it is limited to a municipal entity.

3.   Enforceability of City's interest

Lisa may quiet title nevertheless if the court determines that the city's interest ought not to be enforced. Lisa will argue that the interest ought not to be enforced. She paid market value for the property, and the city paid nothing for their interest. The collateral act, one over which she had no control, creates a windfall in the city. Moreover, the dead hand of Roundhead ought not to be permitted to surface a hundred years after a conveyance. If Roundhead wanted to create a public park he could have done so during his life or at his death by will. The city will argue that the law favors charitable gifts. Moreover, Lisa could only purchase, and therefore probably paid for, only what the railroad held, a limited interest. She likely paid a discounted price. Not to enforce the limitation now creates a windfall in her.

Questions #4-1 and 2

I.   Norris v. City

1.   Validity of ordinance

In order to recover any of the three elements of damages Norris seeks, he must prove that the ordinance is a taking requiring just compensation. He must either prove that the ordinance is not a valid exercise of the police power or, if it is, that its economic impact on his property interest is greater than a private individual should bear without compensation. Both ordinances are valid exercises of the police power. Norris will argue that the city ought not to be able to review their decision not to place restrictions on buildings of less than ten stories. That decision was made in 1990, and nothing has changed since then to warrant application of the standards to buildings of less than five stories. The city will argue that the protection of public from the harm occasioned by earthquakes is a valid exercise of the police power, and it ought to be free to make and revise judgments. In short, the city ought to be able to rethink its public safety policy.

2.   Economic impact on property interest

The revised ordinance may nevertheless be a taking requiring the city to pay Norris just compensation. Ordinarily, only government acquisition of private property triggers the requirement of payment of just compensation under the 5th Amendment. However, takings jurisprudence also applies when government regulation adversely affects a private property owner's interest in her property. Courts look to the character of the invasion and its economic effect. Here the character of the invasion is not physical; there is no permanent occupation of Norris' land. Absent a permanent physical occupation, compensation is required only if his primary economic expectations have been thwarted. He will argue that he intended to build on the site for $50,000,000, and now he must pay $60,000,000. Thus his expectations have been thwarted to the tune of $10,000,000. The city will argue that the increase in cost does not thwart legitimate expectations; businessmen must always factor in cost increases. He intended to build an apartment, and he may do so. The additional costs can be past along to the tenants.

Consequently, Norris cannot retrieve the money paid to the architect. Similarly, he cannot recover his additional $10 million in costs to build the building in compliance with the regulation.

Question #4-3

I. Norris v. City

    1. Takings jurisprudence during moratorium

The city need not pay lost profits during the moratorium. Norris will argue that during the moratorium (five years), his property was rendered valueless. Takings jurisprudence always requires just compensation when land is rendered valueless. The city will argue that the moratorium lasted a reasonable amount of time to allow it to redraft its ordinance. Takings jurisprudence does not allow a landowner to focus on discreet temporal segments to argue that during some period the land was valueless. Moreover, other uses of the land were permitted during that time demonstrating that the argument that the land was rendered valueless is without substance.

PROPERTY ESSAY EXAM #3

Question #1-1

I.   Twolane v. Bonfield

    1.   Copyright protection

The list is not subject to copyright protection. Copyright law rewards the creative process of those who produce writings. Twolane will argue that their employee did not aimlessly engage in internet surfing. Rather, Twolane will argue that 'googling' is a skill, like creating poetry or writing prose, and the fruits of it (gathering addresses) ought to be protected. Bonfield will argue that the creative spark is absent. What was produced was the functional equivalent of a phone book, the compilation of which from public information is not protected.

    2.   Right to publicity

The book is protected by Twolane's right to publicity. Twolane will argue that it markets products for profit under its name, and that it therefore exploits its institutional personality. Courts have protected individuals, usually celebrities, who do the same by creating a common law right of publicity. This book has value because Twolane produces it. As such, all attempts to use their name infringes on that right. Bonfield will argue that the right in common law adhered only to famous individuals, and ought not to extend to institutions, who can defend their intellectual property rights through the traditional categories of copyright, trademark, and patent. Moreover, Twolane is not with the common law right because, it does not market its persona; rather it markets its business.

    3.   Passing off

Is Bonfield passing off his book as the Twolane directory? The law does not permit an individual to sell a different product in such a manner so as to suggest it is the same one that is produced by another. Twolane will argue that Bonfield is misrepresenting the book as the official Twolane directory by creating one very similar, and not making it clear that it is not the official one. This argument Bonfield will reject; the facts make it clear that he merely offering a volume for sale, not the official Twolane directory.

Question #1-2

I.   Twolane v. Bonfield

    1.   Law of capture and finders

Twolane will argue that the law of capture should apply: that the information on alums was similar to a group of wild animals, and that the labor of their employee reduced the information to Twolane's possession. Capture principles have been applied by analogy to property rights other than wild animals, for example minerals. Twolane will argue that the law of capture protects labor, and that their efforts were central to the accumulation of the information. In addition, Twolane will resort to the law of finders: the addresses had been in the possession of the institution, and were lost. Bonfield will argue that neither the law of capture not that of finders should be stretched here. The addresses were neither lost (the institution never had possession of them), nor were they in any sense wild (they were not capable of ownership).

Question #2-1

I.   Zonoroff v. G.W.

    1.   Prescription

By 1992, an easement was created by prescription appurtenant to the mine. An easement can be acquired by prescription where the party so asserting proves open, continuous, and exclusive use of a path with out permission of the titleholder for the period of the statute of limitations. Zonoroff will argue that their use was not concealed, that it was regular, and that it was not undertaken in conjunction with others. Finally, there was not permission given by GW. GW will argue that he was not in residence, and was not aware of the adverse use of the path. This argument will fail: the law requires landowners to monitor the use of their land or suffer the consequences.

Question #2-2

I.   Zonoroff v. GW

1.   Termination through interference with use

The fencing-in and locking of the gate was an attempt to terminate the easement that failed. An easement may be terminated when its use and enjoyment is interfered with in an open, continuous, and notorious fashion, without the objection of the holder of the easement. GW will argue that the lock was a manifestation of his control over the use of the easement, his intention to turn it into a permissive license.

2.   Termination through abandonment

GW will argue that the gating and locking had its desired effect; Zonoroff no longer used the easement. Thus the easement was also terminated by abandonment. Zonoroff will argue that lack of use was not abandonment; he retained the key, and planned to use it when the easement when it was convenient. This argument should prevail, because courts are reluctant to find that individuals voluntarily relinquish valuable property.

3.   Termination by prescription

Zonoroff will argue that it never accepted the act of GW as hostile. Merely giving permission to one who already has right will not transform an easement into a license. The burden is on the landowner to prove permissive use, and GW will be unable to do so.

4.   Exceeding scope of easement

The installation of the wires was beyond the scope of the easement and a timely objection by GW may require removal or a forced sale of the right. By stringing wires over poles, Z has gone beyond the scope of the easement acquired by prescription. GW will argue that this improper use of the easement should terminate the right of way. Z will argue that the offending use creates no greater burden to the land and is therefore within the right of way acquired. However, even if it is not, the entire easement ought not to be terminated, because the improper use (wires) may be separated from the proper use (pathway). Z may argue that an easement for the wires was created by estoppel. The poles and wires were erected under GW's eye, and he did not protest. Having had the opportunity to complain and having failed to do so, he is now estopped from objecting. Z's uncontested activity (a license) occasioned expenditure in reliance; the license is irrevocable. If any compensation ought to be forthcoming, its measure ought to be the decrease in the fair market value of GW's property; that is his loss.

Question #2-3

I.   Zonoroff v. GW

    1.   Obligation to repair easement

Zonoroff will argue that the law requires that the holder of servient interest (the land subject to the easement) to maintain the easement. The road was cut through GW's land; therefore he should be obligated to maintain it. Because he has failed to repair, Zonoroff will argue that he had no alternative but to repair, and he ought to be able to charge the costs to GW's account. GW will argue that most courts permit the holder of the easement to enter the servient estate to repair, a so-called secondary easement. Having exercised the secondary easement by repairing the road, GW will argue that courts should require the party who derives most benefit from the easement to pay the cost. Since Zonoroff uses the road far more frequently than GW, the former should pay the cost of repair. Most courts would support GW's position.

Question #2-4

I.   GW v. Zonoroff

    1.   Exceeding scope of easement

By stringing wires over poles, Z has gone beyond the scope of the easement acquired by prescription. GW will argue that this improper use of the easement should terminate the right of way. Z will argue that the offending use creates no greater burden to the land and is therefore within the right of way acquired. However, even if it is not, the entire easement ought not to be terminated, because the improper use (wires) may be separated from the proper use (pathway). Z may argue that an easement for the wires was created by estoppel. The poles and wires were erected under GW's eye, and he did not protest. Having had the opportunity to complain and having failed to do so, he is now estopped from objecting. Z's uncontested activity (a license) occasioned expenditure in reliance; the license is irrevocable. If any compensation ought to be forthcoming, its measure ought to be the decrease in the fair market value of GW's property; that is his loss.

Question #2-5

I.   GW v. Zonoroff

    1.   Termination and damages for overuse

The excessive use of the easement may be enjoined. GW will argue that when the easement was acquired by prescription, the use was more modest than it now is. Overuse terminates an easement. Z will argue that easements may used consistent with that quantum agreed by the parties. Since this easement was created by prescription, there was no fixed amount of use contemplated by the parties. Therefore, Z may make reasonable use. Reasonable use allows increase in the amount of use made at the time of creation. The court should make a determination of a baseline of reasonable use, and allow GW to regulate Z's use consistent therewith. In addition, GW should be awarded for pecuniary losses occasioned by the overuse.

Question #3-1

I.   Norris v. Corps

    1.   Exercise of police powers

    Norris will claim that the project is not a valid exercise of the police power because it does not protect the public from harm.   Rather it confers a benefit on private landowners at his expense. The Army will claim that such projects do benefit the public in general because they reduce flooding on public land as well, and facilitate the provision of public services in flood prone areas. The Army will argue that it operates pursuant to legislative authority, which is given great deference by courts. The plan by the Army Corp is a valid exercise of the police power.

    2.   Fifth Amendment taking

    The flooding of Norris's land is a taking. Norris will argue that when government conduct requires an individual property owner to suffer a physical invasion, the right to exclude has been taken. Compensation is always required when the invasion is permanent, and here it is arguable whether the water will recede. The Army will argue that the physical invasion is not by individuals, but by water, a natural resource. Compensation is ordered only when entry by an individual is directed. Norris should prevail on that issue, because government conduct is the direct cause of the invasion, and is knowingly undertaken. Moreover, Army will argue that the water will recede, leaving Norris with his land augmented. Whether the land will return is a fact issue, and should be addressed with that of just compensation, rather than liability for a taking.

Question #3-2

I.   Norris v. Corps

1.   Just compensation

Compensation should be limited because the taking is temporary, and there may be some ultimate advantage of the project to Norris and his property. Assuming a taking, Norris must receive just compensation for the property acquired by the government. Norris will argue that the taking decreased his profits. The Army will argue that lost profits are rarely awarded in takings cases. The Army did not acquire his business. The Army will argue that the proper measure of damages is the decreased value of his land: the difference between the fair market value of the property before and after the governmental act. Moreover, the Army will argue that the taking is temporary, and also that Norris's land will eventually increase in quantity. This latter fact gives him reciprocity of advantage that ought to be regarded as a set-off to his claim. Since the loss in value will be potentially for fewer years than the years of gain, minimal or token compensation is warranted. As to the factual issue of whether the water will recede, the court should make Norris await the eventual outcome of the project before conceding more than token compensation.

PROPERTY ESSAY EXAM #4

Question #1

I.   Due v. Shermanfork

1.   Trespasser v. innocent improver

Due will argue that while he was trespassing on Sherman's land, he was in peaceful possession. His occupation was neither violent nor criminal. He ought to be regarded much like an innocent improver. He should receive the value of his labor discounted by some calculation of reasonable rent. Otherwise, Sherman gets a windfall. Sherman will argue that the innocent improver doctrine should not apply to those who know that the land is not theirs. Due is a mere squatter who is accorded no profit of the Lords of his own labor. A trespasser upon land cannot acquire rights in property found on the land

II.   Coward v. Shermanfork

1.   Abandonment

Whether Coward receives the value of the logs or the house depends upon whether the court finds that he abandoned the logs. Coward will argue that since he had purchased the right to fell timber on Sherman's land the logs must be his property. Given the lease, he will argue that so long as the logs are likely to come from the land under lease, a question of fact, the logs should be his property.

2.   Implied Agency

Even if his lumberjacks did not chop down the trees, Due may have and Coward may argue that he did so as his agent. Sherman will argue that the case allows Coward and not trespassers to log, and unless he can prove that his men cut down the logs it should be presumed Due did, unlawfully, and therefore the logs are the property of the landowner. Due cannot be Coward's agent; he wasn't even aware of his conduct. There can be no implied agency; no agreement no agency. Sherman seems likely to get a windfall.

Question #2

I.   Wall v. City

    1.   Exercise of police power

Wall will question the validity of the act. He will argue that the provision of low-income housing is a not a valid exercise of the police power: in what way is harm to the public avoided. What the act does is require him to use his land for the benefit of the public. The act allows the city do satisfy its obligation, to provide low income housing, at Wall's expense rather than at its own expense. If the city requires a low-income housing project, let them build one. The city will argue that there has been no physical invasion of the property. The zoning regulation in question merely regulates land use. Wall can continue to use the property in the manner that it has been used before the fire. Moreover, it provides administrative review in situations in which a variance from its terms is sought. The Low Income Housing Act is a valid exercise of the police power.

    2.   Fifth Amendment taking

Even though it is a valid exercise of the police power, the zoning ordinance may be a taking as applied to Wall's property. Wall will argue that his primary investment backed expectations for his property have been thwarted. He seeks to undertake an otherwise lawful project that will enhance the value of the land value and also benefit the community. Although the premises have been used as low income housing before the fire, investment back expectation should not be frozen in time. His intentions have always been to derive as much return as possible from his land.

The city will respond by noting that his primary intention was to use the property as a low priced hotel, and he can continue to do so. He is still left with a profitable use of land, and he has alternatives that may be even more profitable. He is free to combine housing/non-housing use; and he can also build his cinemas on his land, if he builds low income housing elsewhere.

The city's argument is probably sufficient to prevail.

3.   Board's abuse of discretion

The city planning board may have abuse its discretion by failing to approve the variance. Wall will argue that the fire destroyed the property, and repairs would be costly; therefore, he is within the exception of subsection (a). Moreover, the expense of rebuilding would be regarded as excessive when compared to the potential return. Thus sub-section (c) also applies.

The planning board's discretion is limited to fact-finding, and the facts asserted by Wall clearly meet the legislative mandate. The city will argue that the ordinance states a general prohibition followed by exceptions. The planning board's role is not limit to fact finding. The board has the discretion to determine whether a variance was in order, subject to a general requirement that their decision be made in good faith. Wall's application for a variance was considered and denied.

4.   Measure of damages

Should the court find a taking, the measure of damages should be the difference between the fair market value as unregulated land (the value of the building lot as a potential cinema complex) and the fair market value as regulated (the hotel). Wall will argue that the measure of damages should be his pecuniary loss; lost profits over the time the cinema would operate. The city will argue that a cinema has not been acquired. A use has been curtailed. The measure of damages should be the decreased use value; the difference between the fair market value as unregulated land (the value of the building lot as a potential cinema complex) and the fair market value as regulated (the hotel)

Question # 3

I.   Beatrice v. Jasepea

> 1.   Implied Warranty of Suitability

Jasepea will argue that the landlord knew that he was planning on using the property for a restaurant and that parking was essential. Since the parking lot was common property controlled by the landlord, it was clear that the lease implied a promise to plow. This breach of duty should allow him to quit the premises and be absolved from the obligation to pay rent. Advising Jasepea to move out on the implied warrantly of suitability theory is dangerous because if he does and the court finds for landlord (as it is likely to do) Jasepea is liable for the rest of the lease period..

> 2.   Covenant of Quiet Enjoyment

Jasepea might argue that the landlord breached the covenant of quiet enjoyment. Though usually construed to include prohibitions against affirmative acts by the landlord that interferes with tenant's use and enjoyment, it has also been construed also to include failure to act when there is a duty to act. Thus the failure to plow is a breach of Jasepea's quiet enjoyment. The landlord will argue that the leasehold is still suitable for commercial use; the failure to plow is a minor dereliction, which does not justify damages no less a termination of the lease. Likewise, landlord will argue that even if affirmative duties are implied within the covenant, Jasepea has given inadequate notice of breach. A more appropriate remedy would be "repair and deduct:" get a person to plow and deduct cost from the rent. But advising Jasepea to move out on the constructive eviction theory is dangerous because if he does and the court finds for landlord (as it is likely to do) Jasepea is liable for the rest of the lease period.

II.   Jasepea v. Beatrice

   1.   Landlord tort liability

Jasepea may be able to pass along tort damages should Beatrice sue and prevail. Landlords are not usually liable for torts that occur on demised premises. An exception is recognized for those that occur on property which the lessees enjoy in common. This seems to be the case here. Landlord will argue that Wall and her customers assumed the risk of slippery walks, and that Jasepea should have "repair and deduct", had someone shovel and charge the cost against the rent.

Question #4

I.   Norris v. Jessie

   1.   Adverse possession

Norris may have acquired the 5-foot strip by adverse possession. Norris will argue that for the limitation period of 5 years (according to the statute provided), he used the land open, continuous, exclusive and adverse. He did not conceal his use; the use was uninterrupted by anyone including the titleholder; he did not use it in concert with others, and he claimed it as his right. Jessie will argue that Norris was mistaken as to ownership, and was therefore not adverse. In some jurisdictions, only land that the adverse possessor knows it not his/her own can be adversely possessed. Here Norris was mistaken. Norris will argue that he was an innocent improver; he believed the land was his and should retain the right to possess it. Jesse will argue that he should receive under this theory the decrease in value of his property should the court find that he must grant the 5-foot strip of land to Norris.

2.   Covenant running with the land

The writing executed between Norris and Sal created a real covenant, the burden of which runs with the land to the current titleholder, Jesse. Real covenants are interests in property that may require an owner to do an act or refrain from doing an act on property for the benefit of another property owner. Here Jesse is asked to keep the ditch clean. Jesse will argue that the promise is personal between Norris and Sal and it does not bind him. Norris will argue that the requirements of a real covenant were satisfied. First, there was intent that the premise seen with the land because the writing mentions the heirs and assigns of Sal (Which Jess is). Second the agreement was between those in horizontal property because the two owners (Sal and Norris already had existing covenants — clause 2,345,678) respecting their property. Third Sal and Jesse are in vertical property, because Sal transferred his property to Jesse (Jesse's title search would have revealed the agreement because it was "recorded." Finally, the agreement "touch and concerned" the land, because it conferred a benefit on the land, (indeed a mutual benefit). Jesse's only argument is that there was not intent for the promise to run; heirs and assigns is mere border plate and had Sal expected Jesse to be burdened he would have placed it in the deed.

II.   Jessie v. Norris

1. Covenant running with the land

Jesse can claim that the clause limiting building to within five feet of walls created a real covenant. Norris's only defense would be that the appropriate measure of damages should be monetary damages, and that they are minimal. The alternative of removal would be too costly. Moreover, owners have acquiesced to the beams. An injunction ordering removal should be barred though laches.

2. Nuisance

Jessie may seek removal of the beams in an action in nuisance. For Jesse to prevail in nuisance requires him to prove that the gravity of the harm of the beams to him out weighs their social utility to Norris'. Any other formulation, for example, that the burden is serious (difficult to prove) and Norris can afford to pay its costs is more suited to situations in which the invasion is caused by a commercial enterprise. Indeed it's difficult to "see" the invasion at all. Moreover, Norris's beams occurred before Jesse's purchase; they are "first in time, first in right."

PROPERTY ESSAY EXAM #5

Question #1

I.   Youchello v. Remark and Wall

   1. Found property

   Youchello will argue that he found abandon property, the script, and has rights as against all other claimants. A finder of property, here Youchello, has rights in found property against all persons except the true owner. He will argue that Wall, the author, and arguably it owner, sold the book to Remark, and thereby abandoned his right: he manifested an intention to part with his right. That he never tried to reclaim or use the script is evidence that his sale of the book constituted an abandonment of the script. Youchello will argue that he brought this discarded property back into the stream of commerce, and should be rewarded by receiving the profits from its exploitation.

   Remark will argue that Youchello was an invitee on his premises, but for a limited purpose; he was not invited to find or appropriate any property on the premises. Moreover, he will argue that since he purchased the book, it was under his care in the house, in his constructive possession. Thus it was never lost, and could not be found. The purchase of the book included the purchase of the writing inside. To allow Youchello to reap the profits of exploitation would encourage guests to hunt for windfalls amongst the property of their hosts.

II.   Wall v. Youchello

   1.   Copyright

Wall will argue that copyright law protects the writings of authors. Should he be able to substantiate his authorship, he would claim that the creative spark is his rather than Youchello's and his failure to register his right should not prejudice his right. Copyright in written work extends as least as long as his life. The fact that he did not choose to exploit it until now does not constitute an abandonment of his right. He must, however, somehow argue that he retained some copy of the work for prospective future exploitation. Authors are artists, and may sometimes act eccentrically; that conduct ought not to be regarded as a waiver of his rights.

Question #2

I.   City v. Maseratti

    1.   Validity of ordinance

The zoning ordinance may be challenged as an invalid exercise of the police power. Zoning ordinances are presumed valid, but must be enacted by government pursuant to the police power, the obligation on the part of government to protect the public from harm. On the other hand, Jasepea would question whether harm to the public is created by the building of the tower. At most there might be increased traffic from curiosity seekers. The facts suggest spot zoning, that it was directed at a specific plot of land, or that the governmental act was made in bad faith, for a particular, private rather than public motive. Therefore, it is invalid and unenforceable.

    2.   Equitable servitude

The City Council, on behalf of the landowners, will argue that the restriction created an equitable servitude. Equitable servitudes are use restrictions that bind successive landowners. The City Council would argue that the promise between Luciano and the developer runs with the land. Although not expressly stated in the restriction, the intent to bind successors should be inferred. Residential restrictions only make sense if successor owners are subject to the covenant. They also must touch and concern the land because they must create the mutual burden and benefit of creating residential neighborhoods. If the tower is out of character, and creates traffic, the houses are less valuable as residences.

Jasepea will argue that the clause was personal, a promise between Luciano and the developer, and not one that binds successive owners. He will argue that there are no words suggesting that the restriction binds others; for example, 'heirs and assigns' does not appear. Moreover, he will argue that the restrictions are too vague to be enforced. There is no way of knowing whether or not his tower will affect the 'residential character', or adversely impact property values; some may prefer to live in proximity to the tower, and pay for the privilege. Generally, equitable servitudes must also touch and concern the land. Some economic benefit must accrue to the benefited and burdened lands. As applied to this case, none is apparent. Considering all of these arguments, it is a close call dependent upon whether the court finds the tower to be out of character in a residential neighborhood.

II. Maseratti v. City

1. Validity of ordinance

Jesapea will challenge the ordinance as an invalid exercise of the police power. Zoning ordinances are presumed valid, but must be enacted by government pursuant to the police power, the obligation on the part of government to protect the public from harm. On the other hand, Jasepea would question whether harm to the public is created by the building of the tower. At most there might be increased traffic from curiosity seekers. The facts suggest spot zoning, that it was directed at a specific plot of land, or that the governmental act was made in bad faith, for a particular, private rather than public motive. Therefore, it is invalid, unenforceable, and Jesapea will prevail in obtaining an injunction preventing the application of the zoning ordinance to his tower.

2.   Equitable servitude

Jasepea will argue that the clause in the deed from the developer to Luciano was personal, and does not bind successive owners. Therefore, it is not an equitable servitude which runs with the land. He will argue that there are no words suggesting that the restriction binds others; for example, 'heirs and assigns' does not appear. Moreover, he will argue that the restrictions are too vague to be enforced. There is no way of knowing whether or not his tower will affect the 'residential character', or adversely impact property values; some may prefer to live in proximity to the tower, and pay for the privilege. Generally, equitable servitudes must also touch and concern the land. Some economic benefit must accrue to the benefited and burdened lands. As applied to this case, none is apparent. Considering all of these arguments, it is a close call dependent upon whether the court finds the tower to be out of character in a residential neighborhood.

The City Council, on behalf of the landowners, will argue that the restriction created an equitable servitude. Equitable servitudes are use restrictions that bind successive landowners. The City Council would argue that the promise between Luciano and the developer runs with the land. Although not expressly stated in the restriction, the intent to bind successors should be inferred. Residential restrictions only make sense if successor owners are subject to the covenant. They also must touch and concern the land because they must create the mutual burden and benefit of creating residential neighborhoods. If the tower is out of character, and creates traffic, the houses are less valuable as residences.

3. Notice of equitable servitude

Jasepea will argue that he had no notice of any restrictions when he bought the property in question. A successor must have notice of the burden of an equitable servitude for it to run with the land. While the restriction is not in his deed, the residential character should have put him on notice; he should have looked more carefully at the recorded deeds in his chain of title.

4. Laches

Jasepea will argue that the residents have delayed in seeking a remedy, and the injunction should be denied. He has already made an investment, which would be lost. Damages should be the appropriate remedy, if the neighbors prove a lost in the value of their property. The neighbors will argue that they pursued their remedy expeditiously. The case requires a judgment call on the part of the court.

Question # 3-1

I. Norris v. Stout

1. Common law nuisance

The light may be a nuisance at common law. A nuisance occurs when there is a nontrespassory invasion caused by one individual into the property of another, and on balance the gravity of the harm to the property owner outweighs the social utility to the actor. The light is an invasion of Norris's interest in land. The tougher question is whether the harm is grave — sleep loss is serious, but certainly the birds could be moved at night so they may be silent. On the other hand, perhaps Stout ought to be ordered to move his light; the light need not shine in a particular place to discourage burglars; motion detectors could be installed. Since the burden is on

Norris to prove that on balance the conduct harm outweighs its utility, he may not be able to meet the standard. In short, Norris has other options.

Question #3-2

I.   Norris v. Stout

    1.   Easement by Prescription

Stout may have created an easement in Norris's land by prescription. Open, continuous, exclusive use may give rise to an easement by prescription to have light pass over on to Norris's land. The statutory period of ten years has been satisfied. The issue of adversity is tough. Norris may argue that a ray of light is not sufficient to place an individual on notice that an interest in his property is being acquired. He may be able to argue he permitted it, and therefore it was not adverse, so long as there was no inconvenience. Now that there is a conflict, he objected in a timely fashion. The statute of limitations doesn't run during the permissive period.

Question #4

I.   University v. Sherman

    1.   Deviation from express use limitation

The court should not permit Tulane to terminate the lease and should allow a deviation from the expressed use limitations. Tulane will argue that the law permits tenants and landlords to bargain for restrictions on use in leases. Here the parties limited Sherman's use to only one form of bread: bagels. The court should enforce literally the provision. Sherman will argue that he should be permitted to deviate from the express terms of the lease on the theory of commercial frustration. He will concede that while he agreed to the limitation, it was prior to the health warnings on bagels. He must demonstrate that something beyond his control has effectively rendered the lease commercially impractical. In light of the warnings, nobody will eat bagels; therefore, the purpose of the lease, to sell coffee with bagels, has been frustrated commercially. Moreover, he will argue that it is unreasonable to apply the literal terms of the lease, because the expansion does not affect the landlord's retained property; the addition of croissants does not seem to affect other lessee's businesses, or the operation of the university. Likewise the tutoring of seems to have no undesirable effect on other property and their values. The case would be different if this was a shopping center and a commercial landlord was apportioning use amongst tenants.

II. Sherman v. University

1. Constructive eviction

The interference with the deliveries is a constructive eviction allowing Sherman to quit and terminate the lease, or enjoin Tulane from blocking deliveries. Even if the court does not find commercial frustration, it may be possible for Sherman to rescind the lease and quit the premises claiming a constructive eviction. He will argue that the lease has implied warranty of quiet enjoyment: that the landlord covenants not to undertake acts that interfere with the tenant's use and enjoyment of the premises. Blocking deliveries is just such an act, and it is a substantial interference. All he must do is give notice to the landlord that he intends to vacate because of the landlord's breach. Then prior to suit, he must quit. If his claim prevails, he will be absolved of the rent. If he does not, he will be liable for rent for the rest of the leasehold term, though the landlord may have an obligation to hold the premises open for a replacement tenant.

The landlord will argue that the blockade is not a physical interference with the use and enjoyment of the premises. Landlord's act occurs outside of the actual leasehold property. Moreover, the landlord's will claim that her conduct is undertaken to enforce a legal obligation that Sherman voluntarily undertook.

The court will probably sustain the Sherman's claim. Constructive eviction has been expanded as a tenant's remedy to include actions by the landlord outside of the confines of the premises, and even extended to the acts of the landlord's other tenants. The landlord's conduct seems to be a heavy-handed attempt to enforce the terms of an agreement that ought to be settled by negotiation or litigation.

2. Injunction for changed conditions

If Sherman wishes to continue his business on the leasehold premises, he ought to be able to enjoin the blockade on the grounds that a deviation in the lease terms should be permitted on the commercial frustration theory. Sherman will argue that he should be permitted to deviate from the express terms of the lease on the theory of commercial frustration. He will concede that while he agreed to the limitation, it was prior to the health warnings on bagels. He must demonstrate that something beyond his control has effectively rendered the lease commercially impractical. In light of the warnings, nobody will eat bagels; therefore, the purpose of the lease, to sell coffee with bagels, has been frustrated commercially. Moreover, he will argue that it is unreasonable to apply the literal terms of the lease, because the expansion does not affect the landlord's retained property; the addition of croissants does not seem to affect other lessee's businesses, or the operation of the university. Likewise the tutoring of seems to have no undesirable effect on other property and their values. The case would be different if this was a shopping center and a commercial landlord was apportioning use amongst tenants.

PROPERTY
MULTIPLE CHOICE

100
QUESTIONS

ANSWER SHEET

Print or copy this answer sheet to answer all multiple choice questions.

1. A B C D	26. A B C D	51. A B C D	76. A B C D
2. A B C D	27. A B C D	52. A B C D	77. A B C D
3. A B C D	28. A B C D	53. A B C D	78. A B C D
4. A B C D	29. A B C D	54. A B C D	79. A B C D
5. A B C D	30. A B C D	55. A B C D	80. A B C D
6. A B C D	31. A B C D	56. A B C D	81. A B C D
7. A B C D	32. A B C D	57. A B C D	82. A B C D
8. A B C D	33. A B C D	58. A B C D	83. A B C D
9. A B C D	34. A B C D	59. A B C D	84. A B C D
10. A B C D	35. A B C D	60. A B C D	85. A B C D
11. A B C D	36. A B C D	61. A B C D	86. A B C D
12. A B C D	37. A B C D	62. A B C D	87. A B C D
13. A B C D	38. A B C D	63. A B C D	88. A B C D
14. A B C D	39. A B C D	64. A B C D	89. A B C D
15. A B C D	40. A B C D	65. A B C D	90. A B C D
16. A B C D	41. A B C D	66. A B C D	91. A B C D
17. A B C D	42. A B C D	67. A B C D	92. A B C D
18. A B C D	43. A B C D	68. A B C D	93. A B C D
19. A B C D	44. A B C D	69. A B C D	94. A B C D
20. A B C D	45. A B C D	70. A B C D	95. A B C D
21. A B C D	46. A B C D	71. A B C D	96. A B C D
22. A B C D	47. A B C D	72. A B C D	97. A B C D
23. A B C D	48. A B C D	73. A B C D	98. A B C D
24. A B C D	49. A B C D	74. A B C D	99. A B C D
25. A B C D	50. A B C D	75. A B C D	100. A B C D

PROPERTY QUESTIONS

Question 1 - 4 are based on these facts:

Smith, a second-hand book dealer, purchased a used four-volume set of <u>Blackstone's Commentaries</u> from Jones for $200. Jones inherited the book from his Uncle John. Inside the book, he came across a War Bond made out in the name of Ulysses Wescott, Sergeant, U. S. Army Quartermaster Corp., with a face value of $100. The date of maturity of the bond is January 1, 1950. Even though the bond has matured a half-century ago, the U. S. government continues to be obligated to pay $100. Smith finds out that the value of the bond to collectors is $5,000.

1. How should the property be characterized?

    a.   Lost.

    b.   Mislaid.

    c.   Treasure Trove.

    d.   Abandoned.

2. Before Jones sells the book to Smith, what right does Jones have in the bond?

    a.   True owner.

    b.   Possessor.

    c.   Finder.

    d.   Bailee

3. To whom should the bond be awarded?

a. Smith

b. Jones

c. Wescott if he is alive; his heirs if he is not

d. The U.S. government.

4. Suppose shortly before judgment is entered Smith sells the bond to Banks for $1,000. Banks is unaware of precisely how Smith came to possess the bond. Assume Wescott has died intestate. Wescott's heirs bring an action against Banks and joins Smith.

a. Heirs can collect against Banks and Smith.

b. Heirs can recover against Smith only.

c. She can recover against Banks only.

d. Heirs cannot recover.

Question 5 - 7 are based on these facts:

Smith, an amateur photographer who occasionally sells his travel photos to friends who frame them, recently returned from an "Around the World in 80 days Cruise". He immediately went to his local camera store to get his dozen roles of film developed, and printed. The clerk gave him a receipt for the film. A week later, Smith returned to the camera store, but the clerk was unable to find the prints, the negatives or the exposed film.

5. What legal relationship was created between Smith and camera store?

a. Trust.

b. Bailment.

c. Gift.

d. Conversion.

6. Smith sues the camera store. Which of the following measures of damage can he recover?

a. The value of the film.

b. The value of the photographs.

c. The value of his trip.

d. The cost of a return trip.

7. Suppose the receipt had the following notice in fine print: "Not responsible for lost or damaged film". Which of the following measures of damages can he recover?

a. The value of the film.

b. Sentimental value of the photos.

c. The value of his trip.

d. The cost of a return trip.

Question 8 - 16 are based on these facts:

In 2005, Smith purchased a five acre square tract of undeveloped rural land in the frozen north for $10,000 from Jones who had purchased that land decades ago by quitclaim deed. Smith began to fence off the property. Unbeknownst to either Smith or Jones, Bloggs has used the property each summer as a campsite during his month long vacation for the past 25 years. In the fall

Bloggs also taps what maple trees there are on the land for their sap. Bloggs brings an action to quiet title against Smith. Assume that the state has a twenty-year statute of limitations.

8. Which adverse possession requirement has Bloggs arguably not fulfilled?

    a. Actual possession.

    b. Open and notorious.

    c. Continuous.

    d. Exclusive.

9. Suppose in 1990, ten years after Bloggs entered on to the land, Smith entered the land while Bloggs was tapping the maple trees. Smith tells Bloggs to get off his land, which Bloggs did. Smith then taped some of the remaining untapped trees. The next day Smith posted "No Trespassing" signs. Bloggs returned the following week, and continued her use for the period largely unmolested by Smith, though Smith occasionally tapped the maples in succeeding autumns. Has Bloggs fulfilled the requirements for adverse possession?

    a. Yes, Blogg's entry is no longer adverse.

    b. No, Smith's entry is insufficient to interrupt the continuous requirement.

    c. Yes, Smith's use of the land no longer renders Blogg's use exclusive.

    d. No, Smith's use of the land is minimal and therefore Blogg's use remains exclusive.

10. Suppose in 1995 Bloggs died, and willed all Bloggs's property to Bloggs's daughter, Bloggs, Jr. Bloggs, Jr. continues to use the property as Bloggs did. In 2005, has Bloggs, Jr. fulfilled the 20 years statute of limitations requirements for adverse possession?

    a. No, Bloggs Jr.'s actual possession has not been for the statutory 20 years.

    b. No, Bloggs Jr. may only tack years if she is in privity of estate with the titleholder.

    c. Yes, Bloggs Jr. inherited the property interest that her mother had in the land.

    d. Yes, Bloggs Jr. may add the fifteen years of her mother's possession to her own ten years of possession.

11. Suppose Smith sold the property in 1995 to White. White does not use or monitor Blogg's use of the property. In 2005, Bloggs brings an action to quiet title. Will Bloggs prevail?

    a. Yes, because Smith and White are in privity, Bloggs can tack the years that Smith owned the property to those that White owned the property.

    b. Yes, adverse possession runs against successive owners so long as the underlying requirements are met.

    c. No, Smith and White are not in privity.

    d. No, Smith and Bloggs are not in privity.

12. Suppose Bloggs believed the property was actually owned by her brother during the entire period of her possession. She occupied the property for the 25 years as stated in facts. In 2005, Smith brings an action to eject Bloggs from the premises. How should the court resolve the case?

   a. Against Bloggs if the court requires the adverse possessor to act in 'bad faith' under the so-called Maine rule.

   b. Against Bloggs if the court requires the adverse possessor to act in good faith, under the so-called Iowa rule.

   c. For Bloggs if the court does not take into account the subjective state of mind of the adverse possessor under the so-called Connecticut rule.

   d. All of the above.

13. Smith holds a life estate in Tanacre. Which of the following acts constitutes waste?

   a. He discovers oil on the property, and opens up a mine.

   b. He tears down the residence on the premises.

   c. He tears down the residence on the premises and erects a shopping center.

   d. All of the above.

14. Smith sells Tanacre to Jones with the following limitation: "so long as the property is not used for the sale of alcoholic beverages, but if alcoholic beverages are sold

on the premises the interest in Smith will cease". What interest has been created and/or reserved?

a. Fee simple absolute in Jones.

b. Fee simple determinable in Jones with a possibility of reverter retained by Smith.

c. Fee simple determinable in Jones with a right of entry retained by Smith.

d. Fee simple on a condition subsequent in Jones with a possibility of reverter retained by Smith.

15. At common law, what interest was created when Smith conveyed Tan acre to Jones in the following manner: "to Jones forever"?

a. A fee simple absolute.

b. A fee simple determinable.

c. A life estate.

d. A fee tail.

16. What future interest is created by the following limitation: "to Smith for life, then if Jones survives Smith to Jones, and her heirs".

a. A vested remainder.

b. An executory interest.

c. A contingent remainder.

d. A possibility of reverter.

Question 17 - 25 are based on these facts:

Banks conveys Tanacre as follows: "to Smith for life, then to his daughter Amy for life, then to her children and their heirs, but if Jones passes the bar exam then immediately to Jones". Amy has no children.

17. What future interests are created?

   a. A vested life estate in remainder in Amy; a contingent remainder in her children in fee simple, an executory interest in Jones.

   b. A vested life estate in remainder in Amy; a vested remainder in her children in fee simple, an executory interest in Jones.

   c. A vested life estate in remainder in Amy; a vested remainder subject to open and to divestment in her children in fee simple, an executory interest in Jones.

   d. A vested life estate in remainder in Amy; a vested remainder subject to open in her children in fee simple, an executory interest in Jones.

18. Smith dies. What impact does that have on the state of the title?

   a. Amy's life estate vests.

   b. Amy's life estate becomes a present possessory interest.

   c. Amy takes Tanacre in fee simple absolute.

   d. None of the above.

19. Amy has a child Bertha. What impact does that have on the state of the title?

    a. Amy's life estate terminates.

    b. The executory remainder in Jones is destroyed.

    c. The vested remainder opens to include Bertha.

    d. The contingent remainder vests in Bertha subject to open and divestment.

20. Jones passes the bar. What impact does that have on the state of the title?

    a. Bertha's remainder is divested.

    b. Jones takes Tanacre in fee simple absolute.

    c. Both (a) and (b).

    d. Jones takes Tanacre at the death of Amy.

21. Jones has yet to pass the bar. Amy dies. What impact does that have on the state of the title?

    a. Bertha takes Tanacre in fee simple absolute.

    b. Bertha takes Tanacre until Jones passes the bar.

    c. Bertha takes Tanacre for life.

    d. All of the above.

22. What if thereafter Jones passes the bar?

a. The possessory estate shifts to Jones in fee simple.

b. The possessory estate remains in Bertha in fee simple.

c. Bertha has a life interest only.

d. None of the above.

23. Smith conveys Tanacre to Amy for life, then to Bertha if she reaches the age of 25 for life, then to Carly in fee simple absolute. Bertha is age 20, and Carly is age 18 at the time of the grant. Two years later Carly buys Bertha's interest. What are the consequences of the purchase on the title?

a. None, merger occurs only when two vested estates follow each other.

b. The remainder in Bertha is destroyed, and Carly owns Tanacre in fee simple absolute though merger because she owns a vested life estate and the next succeeding vested interest.

c. The Rule in Shelly's Case creates a fee simple interest in Tanacre in Carly.

d. Under the Doctrine of Worthier Title, Carly owns Tanacre in fee simple absolute.

24. The rule against perpetuities applies to which of the following future interests?

a. Vested remainders

b. Contingent remainders

c. Rights of entry.

d. Reversions

25. Smith conveys Tanacre "to Amy for life, then to Bertha and her heirs when Amy's estate is settled". Does the grant violate the rule against perpetuities and why or why not?

a. No, both Amy and Bertha are alive at the time of the grant.

b. No, Bertha's interest is vested.

c. Yes, Bertha may die before Amy.

d. Yes, Amy's estate may not be settled within the lifetime of Bertha plus 21 years.

Question 26 - 30 are based on these facts:

Smith conveys Tanacre "to Amy for life, and then to Amy's widower for life, then to Amy's issue living at the death of the longer liver of Amy and her spouse". Amy is married to Boris at the time of the grant, and has two children Clare and David.

26. Does the grant violate the rule against perpetuities and why or why not?

a. No, the limitation creates only vested interests.

b. No, Boris, Clare and David are living at the time of the grant.

c. No, although the remainders to the widower and children are contingent, they will vest at the death of Amy, a life in being.

d. Yes, the gift to the widower and to the children are contingent and one or more may vest outside the period of the rule against perpetuities.

27. How might the scrivener have drafted around the rule?

   a. Limit the gift to widower "to Boris".

   b. Limit the gift to a "widower born in the lifetime of Amy".

   c. Limit the gift to a "widower alive at the time of the grant".

   d. (a) and (b).

28. Can a gift be limited to her widower with a remainder to her children and not violate the rule against perpetuities?

   a. Yes, by making the remainder contingent upon the children being alive at the time of Amy's death.

   b. Yes, by making the remainder contingent upon being alive at the time of the surviving widower's birth.

   c. Yes, by making the remainder limited to those living at the time of Amy's death and living at the time for distribution (the death of her widower).

   d. (a) and (c).

29. Would the following reforms of the rule against perpetuities likely save the remainder limited to Amy's children?

    a. The "wait and see" approach.

    b. Cy pres.

    c. The Uniform Statutory Rule Against Perpetuities.

    d. All of the above.

30. Smith conveys Tanacre "to Amy and her brother Boris and the survivor". What estate is created?

    a. A joint tenancy.

    b. A tenancy by the entirety.

    c. A tenancy in common.

    d. Concurrent life estates, with reversion to Smith at the death of the first to die.

Question 31 - 35 are based on these facts:

Smith and Jones have been married for 5 years, and they purchase Tanacre as joint tenants with right of survivorship. They divorce. Smith executes a mortgage on Tanacre in the sum of $40,000 to the Ace Mortgage Company.

31. What effect does the divorce and mortgage have on title to the premises?

    a. The divorce has no effect, but the mortgage severs the joint tenancy.

b. Neither the divorce nor the mortgage has an affect on the joint tenancy.

c. The divorce severs the joint tenancy; the mortgage is secured only on Smith's remaining interest.

d. The mortgage is invalid.

32. During the ten years following the divorce, Smith rents out the property. Smith and Jones share the rent, but Smith pays the taxes, and maintains the premises. At the end of the tenth year, may Smith bring an action against Jones for one-half of the expenses?

a. Smith may be reimbursed for taxes, but not for maintenance.

b. Smith may be reimbursed for maintenance, but not for taxes.

c. Smith may be reimbursed for all expenses paid

d. Smith may be reimbursed for no expenses paid.

33. Smith dies. The mortgage company attempts to foreclose. Absent a statute governing their rights, what should happen?

a. The surviving joint tenant takes the tenancy subject to the mortgage.

b. The surviving joint tenant takes the tenancy free of the mortgage.

c. The mortgage company and Jones hold in joint tenancy.

d. Smith's heirs hold the undivided one-half subject to the debt.

34. In states that recognize common law dower, Smith marries Jones. He purchased Tanacre prior to his marriage, and during the marriage purchased Bronzeacre. They separate. Smith sells both, and dies. What right does Jones have in each property?

a. Jones has dower in Tanacre, but not in Bronzeacre.

b. Jones has dower in Bronzeacre, but not Tanacre.

c. Jones has dower in both.

d. Jones has dower in neither.

35. States that have abolished dower have generally replaced it with the following:

a. Community property system.

b. The elective share.

c. Homestead exemption

d. Uniform Marital Property Act.

Question 36 - 40 are based on these facts:

Smith and Jones are married. Smith is a partner in a law firm. His salary is $75,000 per year, and last year he received a $75,000 bonus. With his bonus, he bought 7,500 shares of XCorp in his own name, and received a dividend of $100. Jones father died this year, and left her a bequest of $100,000. Her salary is $90,000 per year.

36. In a community property state, which of the following items are community property?

   a. Smith's salary.

   b. Smith's bonus.

   c. XCorp dividend.

   d. All of the above.

37. Smith dies in a community property state. In his will, he leaves all his property to the Red Cross. Of the following items, Smith's salary, his bonus and his XCorp dividend, and Jones's inheritance and her salary, which items pass to the Red Cross?

   a. One-half of his share of the community property.

   b. All of his community property.

   c. His earnings, bonus, and dividends.

   d. All, except that Jones get her elective share in his community property.

38. In a common law or separate property state, which items are separate property?

   a. Smith's salary and bonus.

   b. XCorp dividend.

   c. Jones's salary and inheritance.

   d. All of the above.

39. Smith dies in a common law property state. In his will, he leaves all his property (including an inheritance from his mother) to the Red Cross. Of the items mentioned above that are separate property and his inheritance, which pass to Red Cross?

   a. All do.

   b. All do subject to Jones's elective share.

   c. All except his inheritance pass subject to Jones's elective share

   d. One half of all his property does, the other half passes to Jones.

40. Suppose Smith and Jones were unmarried, but they lived together for 20. Which of the following arrangements would allow Smith to pass his estate to Jones at his death?

   a. His will.

   b. A contract to devise.

   c. An *inter vivos* trust naming Smith life beneficiary, with the corpus to pass on his death to Jones.

   d. All of the above.

Question 41 - 43 are based on these facts:

Smith owns a house, and agrees to lease it to Jones. The lease states that it will commence on July 4, 2004, but provides no termination date. Rent reserved is $1,000 per month.

41. What type of tenancy has been created?

   a. A term of years.

   b. A tenancy at will.

   c. A month-to-month tenancy.

   d. A tenancy at sufferance.

42. How can the tenant or the landlord terminate the lease?

   a. Either party can terminate by giving the other party one-month's notice.

   b. Either party can terminate at the end of the one-year lease term.

   c. The tenant may terminate the lease at any time.

   d. The landlord may terminate the lease at any time.

43. Suppose tenant's adult son lives in the house. Tenant dies on September 29th. Tenant wills his entire estate to his son. What are the consequences of tenant's death?

   a. The lease terminates; tenant's son must quit the premises.

   b. Tenant's son may continue to live in the premises as long as he pays the rent, and neither landlord nor tenant's son give notice to quit.

   c. The lease terminates only when the landlord learns of tenant's death.

   d. Nothing.

Question 44 - 45 are based on these facts:

Suppose that the lease reads as follows: "this lease will commence on July 4, 2004 and terminate on January 4, 2005." The rent reserved is $1,000 per month.

44. What type of tenancy has been created?

　　a. A term of years.

　　b. A tenancy at will.

　　c. A periodic tenancy.

　　d. A tenancy at sufferance.

45. How can the tenant or the landlord terminate the lease?

　　a. Either party can terminate by giving the other party one-month's notice.

　　b. Either party can terminate at the end of the lease term.

　　c. The tenant may terminate the lease at any time.

　　d. The lease terminates automatically at the end of the term.

46. On July 1, 2005, Landlord enters the leased premises with his key to show them to a prospective new tenant. Absent a provision to do so in the lease, is the landlord's action wrongful?

   a. No, it is implied in the lease that landlord can show the premises to another prospective tenant.

   b. No, landlords have a general right to inspect the premises.

   c. Yes, the landlord has no right to enter the premises, absent the tenant's consent.

   d. Yes, the landlord's act is not a substantial interference with the tenant's use since the tenant wasn't home.

Question 47 - 48 are based on these facts:

Suppose the lease term is stated as follows: "This lease shall commence on July 4, 2004, and shall terminate immediately at any time by either party giving notice to the other party.

47. What type of tenancy has been created?

   a. A term of years.

   b. A tenancy at will.

   c. A month-to-month tenancy.

   d. A tenancy at sufferance.

48. Suppose tenant's adult son lives in the house. Tenant dies on September 29th. What are the consequences of his death?

   a. The lease terminates; tenant's son must quit the premises.

b. Tenant's son may continue to live in the premises as long as he pays the rent, and neither landlord nor tenant's son give notice to quit.

c. The lease terminates only when the landlord learns of tenant's death.

d. Nothing.

49. Which of the following does the landlord not covenant in a lease?

a. Title

b. Possession

c. Quiet enjoyment.

d. Insurance.

50. If on the day that the lease commences, the previous tenant has not quit the premises, must the landlord take legal action to evict him and place the new tenant in actual physical possession?

a. Yes, in states that have adopted the Uniform Residential Landlord and Tenant Act.

b. Yes, under the common law of most American jurisdictions.

c. No, in states that have adopted the Uniform Residential Landlord and Tenant Act.

d. No, if the demised premises are for a short term furnished residential purposes.

Question 51 - 53 are based on these facts:

Smith leases Tanacre to Jones. The ten-year lease has the following express provision: "the premises must be used for residential purposes as an apartment building". By year eight, the entire surrounding neighborhood has become commercial, and Jones is unable to find residential tenants. Jones asks Smith if he convert the building into a hotel. Smith refuses, and threatens to terminate the lease, and sue for the rent for the remaining term.

51. What would be tenant's best argument in defense?

   a. Impossibility of performance.

   b. Commercial frustration.

   c. Breach of the implied warranty of suitability.

   d. Breach of the implied warranty of habitability.

52. For landlord to prevail in the above claim which of the following would he have to prove?

   a. That the landlord at the time the lease was executed knew that the neighborhood was going 'downhill'.

   b. That it was not reasonably foreseeable at the time the lease was executed that use of the tenancy as apartment would be unprofitable.

   c. That landlord did not know that the neighborhood was declining.

   d. That landlord reasonably believed that using the tenancy as apartments would profitable.

53. What would be the most appropriate remedy if the court found for tenant?

    a. Rescission of the lease.

    b. Reformation of the "express purposes clause".

    c. The difference between the rent reserved and the fair market value of the premises as a residential apartment.

    d. The difference between the rent reserved and the fair market value of the premises as a commercial building.

Question 54 - 56 are based on these facts:

Jones Enterprises owns residential apartments. In their advertisement in the "For Rent" section of the newspaper, they advertise the Smith Arms as a quiet haven in the bustling city. Banks signs a one-year lease. Two weeks after moving in, Banks finds that the noise from his neighbor's television is unbearable.

54. Which of the following tenant's remedies should tenant pursue?

    a. Constructive eviction.

    b. Implied warranty of habitability.

    c. Illegal lease.

    d. Implied warranty of suitability.

55. Which of the following would tenant have to prove to prevail?

    a. That the failure to keep the neighbors quiet was an obligation under the lease.

    b. That the landlord had notice of tenant's objections to the noise.

    c. That tenant moved out in a reasonable time.

    d. All of the above

56. Which of the following would be an appropriate measure of damages should tenant prevail?

    a. Expenses in relocating.

    b. The rental value of the new apartment over the term of the original lease with landlord.

    c. The value of the premises to tenant.

    d. The difference between the rent of a similar apartment without the unruly neighbors and the rent reserved over the term of the original lease with landlord.

Question 57 - 59 are based on these facts:

Suppose after living in the apartment for six-months, the air conditioner no longer functions. Room temperature hovers around 90 degrees. Tenants inform landlord, but landlord fails to repair.

57. Which of the following remedies should tenant pursue?

a. Actual eviction.

b. Implied warranty of habitability.

c. Illegal lease.

d. Implied warranty of suitability.

58. Which of the following would tenant have to prove to prevail?

a. That the failure to fix the air conditioning was an obligation under the lease.

b. That the lack of air conditioning rendered the premises unfit for human habitation.

c. That tenant moved out in a reasonable time.

d. All of the above

59. Which of the following would **not** be an appropriate measure of damages should tenant prevail?

a. Permitting tenant to have the air conditioning fixed, and deducting the cost from tenant's rent.

b. Requiring tenant to pay a reduced rent.

c. The difference between the fair market value of the premises as warranted (with air conditioning) and the fair market value without air conditioning.

d. Allowing tenant relocation expenses.

Question 60 - 61 are based on these facts:

Jones enters into a ten-year commercial lease with Smith Enterprises. The landlord places the following clause in the lease: 'Tenant agrees not to transfer the lease without the written consent of the Landlord". The agreed rent is $5,000 per month.

60. In year six, tenant decides to retire. Tenant wishes to sub-let the premises to X Corp, a large multi-national corporation that plans to use the premises for the same type of commercial enterprise. The landlord refuses to consent, and to explain the reasons for his refusal. Is landlord's action consistent with obligations under the lease?

   a. Yes, the landlord has reserved the right to consent to transfers.

   b. Yes, unless the tenant can allege an oral agreement that limits landlord's right to refuse.

   c. No, regardless of the clause, landlord cannot unreasonably refuse to sub-lease.

   d. No, the lease does not expressly forbid transfers.

61. If the landlord is willing to allow the transfer, should the landlord insist on a sub-let or an assignment?

   a. A sub-let, because then landlord may sue both original tenant Jones and X Corp if the rent is not paid.

   b. A sub-let because landlord may up the rent.

   c. An assignment, because then landlord may sue both original tenant Jones and X Corp if the rent is not paid.

d. An assignment, because landlord may up the rent.

62. For which of the following statements best characterizes landlord tort liability?

    a. Landlords are liable for damages for injuries sustained in common areas.

    b. Landlords are liable for damages for injuries sustained from faulty repairs undertaken.

    c. Landlords are liable for damages for injuries sustained from concealed defects.

    d. All of the above.

63. Under the Restatement (Second) of Torts Sec 821 et. seq., which of the following elements need not be proven by the plaintiff suing in nuisance?

    a. That the plaintiff has an interest in land that has been invaded by the defendant.

    b. That the defendant's act or omission caused an intentional invasion of the plaintiff's interest in land.

    c. That the plaintiff was using her property prior to the point in time in which the defendant began to cause the invasion.

    d. That the defendant's conduct was unreasonable.

Question 64 - 66 are based on these facts:

In 1990, Smith Enterprises erected a brick-making factory three miles from the Town of Bliss. Over the ensuing decade, suburbs of Bliss have now reached the factory's border. Jones purchased property adjacent to the factory, and built her family home on the site. The factory, which only had one shift, has now added an evening shift. Jones brings an action to enjoin the use of the factory entirely or to get damages, because it is noisy, and pollutes.

64. Should plaintiff Jones prevail?

    a. No, there is no invasion of plaintiff's property.

    b. No, the factory was there first.

    c. Yes, the gravity of the harm to plaintiff outweighs the social utility of the factories conduct.

    d. Yes, the harm is serious, but the factory could continue to operate and compensate plaintiff.

65. Should plaintiff's claim prevail, which would be the most efficient remedy?

    a. An injunction against further operation of the factory.

    b. Permanent damages.

    c. Relocation expenses.

    d. All of the above.

66. Suppose the factory agrees to install filters to diminish the output of dust to near zero, but cannot curtail the noise very much given the state of noise abatement technology. In considering whether their

conduct is actionable, which of the following should be considered?

   a. Whether the factory operates according to a fixed schedule.

   b. Whether the factory is operating in good faith.

   c. Whether the factory has made every effort to abate the unreasonable invasion.

   d. Whether noise is an invasion.

67. Which of the following is not an easement?

   a. The right held by the owner of Tanacre to cross Bronzeacre to reach her garage.

   b. The right held by the owner of Tanacre to prevent the owner of Bronzeacre to use her land for commercial purposes.

   c. The right of the owner of Tanacre to use a drive partly on her own land and party on the land of Bronzeacre.

   d. The right of a person to fish in Bronzeacre Lake.

Question 68 - 72 are based on these facts:

Smith and Jones are adjoining landowners. A dirt road has long been located on Smith's land, about four feet from the boundary between the two plots. Five years ago, Jones decided to construct a house on her previously vacant lot. Jones asked Smith if her construction team could use the road for building equipment access. Smith agreed. The road was used during the building of her house. Jones continued to use the road for day-to-day access, and last year Jones asked Smith if Jones could pave it at Jones's own expense. Shortly thereafter Jones had the road paved. Last month, Banks bought Smith's land and blocked Jones's access.

68. If an easement was indeed created, how was it created?

   a. By grant.

   b. By prescription.

   c. By necessity.

   d. By estoppel.

69. If an easement was created, can Banks' enjoin Jones's use?

   a. No, the burden of the easement runs with Smith's parcel.

   b. No, the benefit of the easement runs with Jones's parcel.

   c. Yes, the burden is personal, it can only be enforced against Smith.

   d. Yes, the benefit terminated when Smith sold his land to Banks.

70. If an easement was created, can Jones's guests also use the drive to reach her house?

   a. Yes, if such use was in the contemplation of Smith and Jones when they agreed to her use of the drive.

b. Yes, if Jones's guests had used the drive while Smith owned the servient parcel.

c. No, only the holder of an easement can use an easement.

d. No, easements are personal.

71. Suppose Banks now also decides to buy Jones's parcel. He then grants the same parcel to Norris without mentioning the easement. Is the original Banks' parcel subject to the easement?

a. No, the easement was terminated by merger when Banks held both the original Smith and Jones parcels.

b. No, unless Banks was using the drive to reach the land previously owned by Jones.

c. No, the easement was not mentioned in the grant to Norris.

d. Yes, easements run with the land.

72. Suppose that before selling Jones decides to use her parcel for commercial purposes. She builds a group of five small hunting lodges on her parcel. The huntsfolk use the drive. Which of the following arguments might Banks (owning the original Smith parcel) successfully use to stop them?

a. The easement was terminated by misuse.

b. Excessive overuse terminates an easement.

c. Use beyond the scope of the easement can be enjoined.

d. The easement was terminated by merger.

73. Which of the requirements for the creation of an easement by implication are not required for the creation of an easement by necessity?

a. Unity of title.

b. Severance.

c. Necessity.

d. Apparent use so as to constitute notice.

Question 74 - 79 are based on these facts:

Joes's Bar has operated in the same premises for the past 40 years. Business is good, and Joe wants to move three blocks north to a larger venue. He conveys the building he owns to Banks and places the following restriction in the deed: "vendee agrees not to use the premises as a bar".

74. Banks uses the premises as a flower shop. Business is not good and a year later he opens up a bar. Joe sues to enjoin the use of the premises as a bar. How would he characterize the limitation?

a. An equitable servitude.

b. A possibility of reverter.

c. A right of entry for condition broken.

d. An easement.

75. If Jones sued Banks to enjoin Banks from using the premises as a bar, which of the following would be Banks' best argument in defense?

    a. He was not in horizontal privity with Joe.

    b. He was not in vertical privity with Joe.

    c. The covenant does not touch and concern the land.

    d. The promise was not mutual.

76. Suppose instead of using the premises as a bar, Banks sold the premises to Norris who uses the premises as a bar. May Joe enjoin Norris's use?

    a. Yes, if the requirements of an equitable servitude are met.

    b. Yes, if the restriction was intended to bind successors.

    c. No, there is no privity between Norris and Banks.

    d. No, there is no privity between Joe and Norris.

77. Could Joe sue Norris for damages in the amount of his lost profits occasioned since Norris opened his bar?

    a. No, equitable servitudes are enforced only through injunctions.

    b. No, there is no privity between Norris and Banks.

    c. Yes, if the elements of a real covenant can be met.

    d. Yes, covenants not compete can be enforced as equitable servitudes in an action for damages

78. Suppose Joe decides to pursue a remedy at law. Which of the following may Norris raise in defense?

   a. That covenants to compete do not touch and concern, a requirement for the enforceability of a promises against successors as a real covenant.

   b. That the covenants not to compete are always personal.

   c. That covenants not to compete can only be enforced against the promisor.

   d. That Norris and Joe are not in horizontal privity.

79. Suppose Joe sells his new bar to Manny who sells to Moe. Can Moe enforce the promise against Norris as either a real covenant or an equitable servitude?

   a. No, only the original promisee can enforce promises that run with land.

   b. Maybe, successors in interest to promisees can enforce promises against successors in interest to promisors if the requirements of a real covenant or equitable servitude are met.

   c. Yes, so long as the touch and concern requirement is met.

80. Which of the following planned uses for land might not pass the "public use" tests set out by the Supreme Court in establishing guidelines for the exercise of eminent domain?

   a. A post office.

b. A state courthouse.

c. A multiuse urban renewal project.

d. All of the above.

81. For which of the following would Joe of Joe's Bar above **not** be compensated for if his land was taken by eminent domain to build a highway?

a. The fair market value of the parcel taken.

b. The fixtures on the parcel.

c. Relocation expenses and lost profits during the relocation period.

d. The fair market value of the building on the premises.

82. Suppose Joe owned the bar in fee simple, but leased it to Manny. Ten years remained on the lease. Who would receive just compensation and for what interests?

a. Joe takes the entire amount.

b. Manny takes the entire amount.

c. Joe and Manny divide the amount; Manny receives the value of the lease, and Joe the remaining value.

d. Joe and Manny divide the amount; Joe gets the value of property and Manny gets the value of the fixtures.

83. Under what circumstances does a government regulation always require that the landowner be paid just compensation?

    a. Where there is an average reciprocity of advantage.

    b. Where the government conditions the approval of a use of the premises, but requires the landowner to grant some benefit to the public.

    c. Where the regulation requires a permanent physical occupation of the land.

    d. Where the value of the land has been reduced by the regulation.

Question 84 - 88 are based on these facts:

Smith bought a large beachfront tract of land on a barrier island off the coast of Atlantis in 1995. He bought the property to build a single-family dwelling on the premises. A year or so later as lot prices climbed, he thought about sub-dividing the land into two beachfront lots, a proposal that did not require permission. He dithers. In 2004, Atlantis passed a law that prohibited, amongst other things, the sub-division of any lots on the beach. The prohibition lasts two years.

84. Smith brings action in federal court claiming that a regulatory taking has occurred. Which argument best supports his takings claim?

    a. His primary expectations have been thwarted.

    b. The use of his land, two houses, was not regarded as a nuisance at common law.

c. A two-year prohibition is tantamount to a permanent taking of his right to develop.

d. Not being able to sub-divide is tantamount to the government occupying one-half of his land.

85. Suppose instead of preventing the sub-division, Smith was permitted to sub-divide, but was required to deed a strip of land to the public for access to the beach. Which argument best supports a takings claim?

a. The requirement would be an unconstitutional condition and therefore requires just compensation because sub-dividing his land does not make it more difficult for the public to access the beach.

b. The requirement requires just compensation because it thwarts his investment-backed expectations.

c. The requirement requires just compensation because the public is in possession permanently of part of his land.

d. The requirement requires just compensation because the strip of land has been rendered valueless to him.

86. If Smith was able to place a gate on the strip, and allow access only on an occasional basis when the beach public beaches were crowded, what argument might the government make to support their claim that there was not taking?

a. That there was no taking of the strip because Smith could control time, place, and manner of public access.

b. That there was no taking of the strip because the gate gave him an average reciprocity of advantage.

c. That there was no taking of the strip because Smith's investment backed expectations were now preserved.

d. That there was no taking of the strip because Smith's land lost no value.

87. Euclid v. the Village of Ambler is the central case in zoning law for which of the following reasons?

a. It upheld the constitutionality of Ambler's zoning master plan as applied to property owned by Euclid.

b. It determined that the principle of zoning was a valid exercise of the police power and therefore some limitation on use might not be a taking.

c. It determined that zoning plans may devalue some private property rights.

d. It questioned whether particular parcels of Euclid's land had been taken without just compensation.

88. Smith has run a convenience store on unzoned land. The town zoning board reclassified his property, and that of neighboring businesses as "Low income residential" last month. Which factors should a zoning board **not** take into account in determining whether and for how long each business affected may operate as a non-conforming use?

a. The value each property.

b. The social utility of the business affected.

c. Height and density of the structures.

d. The proximity of the store to other stores.

89. What response best describes the United States Supreme Court's most recent pronouncements on the state or municipalities ability to zone out adult bookstores/entertainment venues?

a. A community may zone adult bookstores/entertainment venues into high crime areas.

b. Zoning as applied to adult bookstores/entertainment venues triggers strict scrutiny.

c. Zoning as applied to adult bookstores/entertainment venues triggers loose scrutiny.

d. Zoning as applied to adult bookstores/entertainment venues triggers an intermediate level of scrutiny.

90. Which of the following zoning ordinances should be held invalid?

a. Those that prohibit unrelated individuals from living together in areas zoned single family residential only.

b. Those that exclude multi-generational families from living together in areas in areas zoned single family residential only.

c. Those that exclude sorority sisters from living together in areas in areas zoned single family residential only.

d. Those that prohibited members of a religious community from living together with families in areas zoned single family residential only.

91. Which of the following is true of zoning plans that exclude provision for low-income housing?

   a. They violate the equal protection clause of the United States Constitution.

   b. They violate the Fair Housing Act.

   c. They violate the constitution of most American states.

   d. They violate the construction of a few American states.

92. Which of the following need not be proved in order to receive a variance from a zoning regulation?

   a. The granting of the variance would not be incompatible with the comprehensive plan.

   b. The landowner will suffer a unique hardship owing to the zoning.

   c. The landowner holds the only lot that will be detrimentally affected.

   d. The hardship is unnecessary because it will not be suffered if the variance is granted.

Question 93 - 95 are based on these facts:

On July 4, 2003 Smith orally agreed to purchase Tanacre from Jones for $5,000 on July 30th. Jones agreed to produce a contract for sale by the 14th. The following day Smith posted a check to Jones in the amount of $2,500. Smith then approached Bank Zero for a loan commitment for $4,000 secured on the premises. On the 14th, Jones tore up Smith's check and signed a contract with Norris to sell Tanacre for $6,000.

93. May Smith sue Jones for damages?

   a. No, the transaction does not satisfy the Statute of Frauds.

   b. No, a seller can always refuse to close until a contract is signed.

   c. Yes, receipt of the deposit precludes a sale to a third party.

   d. Yes, Smith, having partially performed his obligations, equity will order specific performance.

94. Suppose when Smith sent the check to Jones he wrote on the reverse of the check the following: "Deposit for one-half the purchase price of Tanacre, remaining sum to be paid to by closing July 30th subject to financing". Does the check satisfy the Statute of Frauds?

   a. Yes, it contains all the essential information required by the Statute.

   b. Yes, the receipt of the check with a summary of the agreed terms satisfies the Statute.

   c. No, Jones not having cashed the check, there is no unequivocal indication that the seller has agreed to the terms set out on the reverse of the check.

d. No, a deposit check can never constitute a sales contract under the Statute because it is signed only by the buyer.

95. Which of the following would have to have occurred to make the oral agreement enforceable?

a. Jones cashed the check.

b. Smith paid Jones the entire sale price in cash before the contract with Norris was signed.

c. Smith signed a contract with a builder, Banks, to build a house on Tanacre.

d. Smith's builder entered into the premises and began to construct the house.

96. Suppose instead of the above arms length transaction, Smith had agreed to care for Jones for the rest of Jones's life, in return for an option to buy the property for $2,000 less than appraised fair market value at Jone's death. Would this oral agreement be enforceable at Jones's death assuming performance by Smith?

a. Yes, the Statute does not apply in respect of partially gratuitous transfers.

b. Yes, equitable estoppel applies.

c. No, the terms of the oral agreement are not specific as to price.

d. No, the agreement violates public policy.

97. After the sales contract for purchase of residential property, which of the following circumstances, if undisclosed by the seller, would make the title no longer "marketable"?

    a. All deeds in the chain of title have residential restrictions.

    b. All deeds in the chain of title have single family dwelling only restrictions.

    c. The property is zoned single family residential.

    d. The house on the property does not meet building code standards.

98. Which of the following defects in deeds would render title not marketable?

    a. A previous deed in the chain of title misdescribes the property subject to the contract.

    b. The guardian of the minor titleholder has executed a previous deed in the chain of title, and the minor has not joined.

    c. A previous deed in the chain of title includes a testamentary transmission.

    d. A previous deed in the chain of title has a corporate owner, and only an officer has executed the deed.

Question 99 - 100 are based on these facts:

On July 4th, 2003, Smith as vendor and Jones as vendee enter into a contact to for the sale of Tanacre. Jones pays a down payment of one-third the purchase price of $100,000.

99. Two weeks later, a mudslide destroys the house and the lot uninhabitable. If Jones refuses to close may Smith seek specific performance?

   a. Yes, in most states under the doctrine of equitable conversion.

   b. Yes, but only if was unaware that the property was susceptible to mudslides.

   c. No, unless Smith misrepresented the topography.

   d. No, in most states under the doctrine of equitable conversion.

100. Suppose the mudslide occurs and renders both the house and lot uninhabitable. Which of the following would preclude a claim by Smith for specific performance?

   a. There was a clause allowing the buyer to void the contract if the premises were damaged by an act of God.

   b. Smith continued to hold a casualty insurance policy on the premises.

   c. Jones had taken out a casualty insurance policy on the premises.

   d. Jones had taken out a casualty insurance policy on the premises to commence on the closing date.

PROPERTY
MULTIPLE CHOICE

ANSWERS &
ANALYSIS

PROPERTY ANSWERS AND ANALYSIS

1. **Issue: Characterization of Property.**
    Answer (b) is the correct answer. The property should be characterized as mislaid. Because people generally do not part with valuable property, courts rarely find property to be 'abandoned'(d), (owner voluntarily relinquishes her right). The property, though old, is not that old, and was not found in the ground; hence it is unlikely to be considered 'treasure trove'(c). Because it must have been placed in the book, it was not 'lost', where possessor or owner accidentally loses possession. The property was mislaid, because the circumstances in which it was found suggest that it was placed in the book, and forgotten by the owner.

2. **Issue: Characterization of rights by holder.**
    Answer (b) is the correct answer. Jones is a possessor. Ownership of the book, rather like ownership of land, conveys constructive possession of that which is within the pages. The true owner of the bond is Sergeant Westcott, or if he is dead, his heirs or legatees (a). Jones is not a finder, because he never seems to have been aware that the bond was in the book (c). He is not a bailee (d) because a possessor did not voluntarily deliver property to him.

3. **Issue: Priority of rights.**
    Answer (c) is the correct answer. The court should award the bond to Wescott or his heirs. The finder of property, here Smith, has rights against all but the true owner. Having paid value for the bond, Westcott is or was the owner (a). If he is dead, it ought to go to his heirs. The U. S. government (d) has no right in the bond; it is merely Westcott's debtor. While Jones has a right in the property as a prior possessor(b), his right is inferior to that of the true owner.

4.   **Issue: Rights of bona fide purchasers.**

Answer (b) is the correct answer. Wescott or his heirs may recover against Smith, but not Banks. Banks (a) and (c) is a bona fide purchaser for value, and therefore has good title under Uniform Commercial Code sec. 2-403(1). Smith did not come into possession of the property wrongfully; he therefore had at least voidable title, allowing him to pass good title to one who believes he is purchasing from an individual with good title. But since Wescott had a greater right in the property than did Smith, and he attempted to assert it, he ought to be able to recover against Smith.

5.   **Issue: Creation of bailments.**

Answer (b) is the correct answer. A bailment has been created. A bailment is a voluntary transfer and delivery by a possossor of property (bailor) to another (bailee) for safekeeping, and with the expectation that the property would be returned. Smith expected both printing and return of the film negatives. It was not a gift (c) because, though there was delivery, there was no donative intent; neither party believed that the camera shop would keep the negatives. A trust (a) was not created; trusts are created when a party expressly undertakes a fiduciary obligation to hold legal title for the benefit of a third party. There was no intent expressed to create a trust; no words establishing a trust were used. Conversion occurs when a party exercises ownership right over the property of another without consent (d). Here Smith voluntarily handed over the film.

6.   **Issue: Bailor's remedy for loss of bailed property.**

Answer (a) is the correct answer. Smith will certainly be able to claim (a) and possibly (b). In bailments, the bailor expects the return of the property bailed. Generally, bailees are strictly liable for failure to redeliver bailed property. So the bailor must only redeliver the undeveloped film? Not in this case. An exception is made where the bailor expects the property to be processed. Here Smith handed over exposed film; he expected the return of a processed product: negative and prints. Absent agreement, bailees are not responsible for consequential damages; thus he cannot receive either the value of his trip (c) or a return trip (d).

7.   **Issue: Bailee's disclaimer.**
     Answer (a) is the correct answer. The camera shop may still be liable for (a). The camera store attempted to limit its liability in the event it lost or damaged the film. They will argue that the bailment was subject to the express condition. While courts may enforce the exculpatory clause, it may not absolve the camera store from negligent conduct. Thus the standard may be altered from strict liability to negligence. Losing the film while in the store probably meets that standard.

8.   **Issue: Continuous use.**
     Answer (c) is the correct answer. For a possessor to perfect a clam of adverse possession, adverse possessor's occupation must be actual, open and notorious, continuous exclusive, and adverse. Because she has made an entry onto the land she is in actual possession (a). Her possession is open and notorious (b) because she has made no attempt to conceal it, so that a reasonably vigilant owner would know of her entry. It is exclusive (d) because she does not appear to be using the property in concert with others or with the titleholder. However, it may not be continuous because she uses the property seasonally, rather than for the entire year.

9.   **Issue: Adverse possession.**
     Answer (c) is the correct answer. Even a brief period of use by the land titleholder is generally held sufficient to break both the continuous

requirement for adverse possession. Arguably the titleholder is monitoring his land, by posting "No Trespassing" signs. By exercising his ownership rights, Smith has made clear he intends to protect his right in the land.

10.   **Issue: Tacking.**
Answer (d) is the correct answer. Successive possessors may tack years of possession to reach the statute of limitations if the successive possessors were in privity of estate. In order to meet that requirement, possession has to be transferred from one possessor to the next through a legally recognized transfer such as a contract for sale, gift, or a will. Thus the fifteen years Blogg's held can be used by Bloggs, Jr. to meet the 20 year limitation. While it is true that Bloggs Jr. may have 'inherited' (c) the years Bloggs had accumulated, it is the concept of tacking that allows Bloggs Jr. to add them to her own years of possession to meet the statutory period. It is not correct to say that she has not met the requirements for tacking (a) and (b).

11.   **Issue: Change of land ownership.**
Answer (b) is the correct answer. Tacking (and therefore privity) is only necessary when adverse possessors come and go, not when the property is transferred (c) and (d). Adverse possession observes the conduct of the adverse possessor: has her conduct met the standard of actual possession, open, notorious, continuous, exclusive, and adverse. If the titleholder does not to protect his right, adverse possession is perfected. So long as the subsequent owner of the property had a reasonable time period to object to the adverse possessor's use of the land, the adverse possessor may bring an action to quiet title against the second owner.

12.   **Issue: Adversity requirement.**
Answer (a) is the correct answer. Most courts delve into the state of mind of the adverse possessor. Under the Maine rule, the adverse possessor must be subjectively hostile; she must know the property is not hers. Here Bloggs actually believes that she is occupying the land of her brother, presumably with his permission and therefore is not hostile or adverse. Other jurisdictions require subjective good faith: that the occupier has reason to believe that she has a legal right in the property. Merely, thinking the property is her brother's is insufficient unless she has some objective basis. Thus Blogg's in not acting in 'good faith' under the Iowa formulation (b). A third group of jurisdictions do not delve into the occupier's intent; they find the adversity requirement fulfilled by the objective fact of occupation (c). Under this last formulation, Bloggs would prevail.

13.   **Issue: Waste.**
Answer (d) is the correct answer. A life tenant has a limited interest in the tenancy, and must deliver the premises to the reversioner or remainderman in the same condition as she received it. Another way of characterizing the obligation is that the life tenant may not undertake acts that devalue the premises. In each example, the value of the premises is diminished. The oil is no longer an element of value in the land (a); nor is the residence (b). Arguably the shopping center is an improvement; but because at the time that the residence is torn down, the positive economic effect is speculative, the act still constitutes waste (c).

14.   **Issue: Defeasible fees.**
Answer (b) is the correct answer. There are two types of conditional fee simple estates in land: the fee simple determinable, and the fee simple on a condition subsequent. They differ from the fee simple absolute (to A and her heirs) in that the

grantor has subjected the estate to a use limitation (a). While the words actually used frequently direct the categorization of the conditional fee (fee simple determinable "so long as", fee simple on a condition subsequent "but if"), the real issue is whether the grantor provided for an automatic cessation of the interest of the grantee, and return of the estate to the grantor or her heirs, or an optional one, that the grantor may re-enter the premises, and take the possessory interest from the grantee if he so desires. Here the words suggest automatic rather than optional cessation (d), and therefore a fee simple determinable in Jones with a possibility of reverter in Smith, and not a right of entry (c).

15. **Issue: Fee simple absolute.**

Answer (c) is the correct answer. In order to create a fee simple absolute, the grantor was required to use the proper words of limitation: to Jones and his heirs (a). Failure to so would vest a present possessory life estate in the grantee. Creation of a fee simple determinable occurred when the grantor subjected the property to a use limitation (b). A fee tail required the use of the limitation to Jones and the heirs of her body (d).

16. **Issue: Future interests.**

Answer (c) is the correct answer. The interest in Jones is contingent remainder. It is limited to take effect at the time it is created on the occurrence of an event that is uncertain: the survival of Jones at the death of Smith. A remainder is vested if it is limited to a specified person, on the occurrence of an event certain to occur (to A for life, than to B) (a). Executory interests do not take effect upon the natural termination of a simultaneous created estate (to A, then to B at 21) (b). Possibility of reverters are created when the grantor limits a fee simple determinable (d).

17. **Issue: Future interests.**
    Answer (a) is the correct answer. Amy has a vested life estate in remainder (the limitation is to a certain person, Amy, to become possessory on an event certain to occur, the death of Smith); no event need occur for her to enjoy the estate so it is not contingent. Her children as yet unborn have a contingent remainder; the limitation is uncertain persons, to children unborn, and perhaps never born. Thus any response (b) through (d) is incorrect. Jones interest is an executory interest and not a contingent remainder (contingent upon passing the bar), because it will cut short an interest, and not become possessory at the natural termination of a simultaneously created estate.

18. **Issue: Future interests.**
    Answer (b) is the correct answer. Amy's vested remainder becomes a present possessory estate at the termination of its supporting estate. But the quality of her estate is an estate for her life as specified in the limitation. The remainder was already vested, because the limitation is to a certain person, Amy, to become possessory on an event certain to occur, the death of Smith (a). A fee simple absolute endures forever, and not for the life of an individual (c).

19. **Issue: Future interests.**
    Answer (d) is the correct answer. The birth of Bertha causes the contingent remainder to vest both subject to open (in the event that Amy has further children) and subject to divestment (in the event that all her children predecease her). The birth of Bertha has no effect on the interests of Amy or Jones. These interests endure or fail according to their own terms (a) and (b).

20. **Issue: Future interests.**
    Answer (c) is the correct answer. Under the terms of the limitation, the interest in Jones, the

executory interest immediately becomes possessory upon passage of the bar. Thus the vested remainder subject to divestment and open is divested, and the possessory estate in Amy is terminated immediately; she does not continue to enjoy it until her death (d).

21. **Issue: Future interests.**
Answer (a) is the correct answer. Upon the death of Amy, the vested remainder subject to divestment and open vests and closes, and becomes a possessory fee simple absolute in the described taker, Bertha. The divesting condition, the death of Amy without issue, has not occurred. The remainder cannot remain open, because Amy, now deceased, cannot have further issue.

22. **Issue: Future interests.**
Answer (b) is the correct answer. It is too late for Jones (a). The limitation requires that condition of the executory interest (Jones passing the bar) occur before the estate in the children of Amy becomes a possessory fee simple absolute. Jones did not meet the condition and Bertha takes the estate in fee, and not only for her life (c).

23. **Issue: Merger.**
Answer (b) is the correct answer. Merger occurs when the same person holds a vested estate and the **next succeeding** vested estate (not next (a)). When Carly buys Any life interest she holds a vested life estate, and a vested remainder, with a contingent estate between the two. Merger of the two vested estates squeezes out Bertha's contingent interest. Neither the Rule in Shelley's Case nor the Doctrine of Worthier Title apply. The first applies when a conveyance grants a life estate to Amy and a remainder to her heirs (c). The grant in the question creates a fee simple in Amy. The latter holds that when a grantor makes a grant of a life interest wit a remainder to the grantor's heirs, the

grantor heirs take nothing and retains a reversion (d).

24. **Issue: Rule against perpetuities.**
Answer (b) the correct answers. The rule against perpetuities applies only to contingent interests. Reversions, (d) rights of entry (c) and vested remainders (a) are considered vested interests.

25. **Issue: Rule against perpetuities.**
Answer (d) is the correct answer. Amy has a vested life estate; Bertha a springing executory interest in fee simple. The latter must vest or fail within the period of the rule, a life in being plus 21 years. Though unlikely, Amy could die, grief- stricken Bertha could die the following day, and the slothful executor might take more than 21 years to probate the estate. Thus the act that causes the interest to vest **might** vest longer than a life in being plus 21 years. That Bertha is dead is irrelevant: the interest is in fee simple, and would vest in the heirs of Bertha if she was dead at the time the interest becomes possessory.

26. **Issue: Rule against perpetuities.**
Answer (d) is the correct answer. Both interests are contingent, and therefore the entire limitation violates the rule against perpetuities *ab initio.* They take effect to uncertain persons, a widower, and children living at the time of the death of Amy and the widower. Although Boris is alive, he may die, and Amy may marry a man, Edgar, who is not born the time of the grant. While the gift to him must vest or fail on the death of Amy, a life in being, the gift to the children vests at his death, which may occur more than 21 years after a life in being at the time of the grant. Clare and David may die, and after the grant Amy may have a son Frank. Edgar survives Amy, Clare, and David by more than 21 years.

27. **Issue: Rule against perpetuities.**
    Answer (d) is the correct answer. By having the remainder limited to a person now living, the widower and Amy can be measuring lives. The remainder in the children then living must vest or fail in their lifetimes. The limitation to a "widower born in the lifetime of Amy" doesn't help. First she must marry someone alive in her lifetime, and secondly, the perpetuities period runs from the time of the grant.

28. **Issue: Rule against perpetuities.**
    Answer (d) is the correct answer. Remainders may be limited to children yet unborn, so long as they vest within a life in being and 21 years. In order for the children's remainder to fall within the perpetuities period, they must vest or fail at Amy's death as in (a) or (c). Choice (a) allows Amy's children to will away their remainder interest, while choice (b) distributes only to those living at the time for distribution.

29. **Issue: Rule against perpetuities.**
    Answer (d) is the correct answer. Only a handful of states retain the rule in it pristine form. The rule against perpetuities invalidates all future interests in a grant if any interest in the limitation violates the rule. Under the "wait and see" approach interests are given effect if they vest during the perpetuities period (a). In the example above, the interest in Amy's children would not fail unless she married a spouse who was born after the grant. Under cy pres, the court would construe the limitation as granting the remainder to only spouses born at the time of the grant (b). The USRAP sets a time period, usually about a century for contingent interests to vest, a likely occurrence here (c).

30. **Issue: Joint tenancy.**
    Answer (a) is the correct answer. Courts would

probably conclude that a joint tenancy has been created. Joint tenancies are a particular form of concurrent ownership in each party owns an undivided half interest; at the death of the first joint tenant to die, the survivor owns the entire interest. Usually the word of art "with right of survivorship" appears in the limitation, but the words used here are sufficient to suggest that the survivor should own the tenancy. A tenancy by the entirety is a particular type of joint tenancy between spouses (b). A tenancy in common is a joint ownership arrangement in which the surviving joint tenant does not take the deceased's undivided half share (c). Thus the use of the word "survivor" does not suggest a tenancy in common.

31. **Issue: Joint tenancy.**
    Answer (b) is the correct answer. Unmarried individuals can hold property in joint tenancy; the divorce has no effect on the title. Even without consent, a mortgage undertaken by a joint tenant does not sever the joint tenancy (a), because in most states, the title to the mortgage property remains with the mortgagor, and the debt is a lien on the property. Severance would only occur on foreclosure. In some states, however, the mortgagee does take title subject to the mortgagor's equity of redemption. In these states (few in number), title is no longer in the joint tenants, but courts in these jurisdictions recognize the ownership in the mortgagee as a legal fiction.

32. **Issue: Joint tenancy.**
    Answer (a) is the correct answer. Joint tenants are responsible for their share of the tax liability of the joint tenancy. Taxes are an obligation on the owners. However, the joint tenant is not obligated to repair, or to pay other expenses (b) (c) or (d); if Smith does so Smith cannot charge the other joint tenant.

33.   **Issue: Joint tenancy.**
Answer (b) is the correct answer. Because the undivided half interest of the mortgagor no longer exists, the mortgage company has no recourse in a lien theory state. The debt does not pass to the survivor when the interest of the deceased joint tenant passes (a), because legally speaking the deceased joint tenants interest doesn't pass (c). The deceased's undivided half ceases to exist, as does the secured debt (d). For this reason it is prudent for a lender to have both joint tenants take out the mortgage.

34.   **Issue: Dower rights.**
Answer (c) is the correct answer. At common law, dower attaches to all property real property that the husband was seised of at anytime during marriage. Unless the wife released her dower, she has a right to the dower in both parcels.

35.   **Issue: Dower rights.**
Answer (b) is the correct answer. In most jurisdictions, the elective share has replaced dower. Both real and personal property are subject to the elective share. Eight states have the community property (a) system, derived from continental jurisdictions in which dower was not present. Only Wisconsin has adopted the UMPA (d). The homestead exemption is a right granted to the surviving spouse to live in the marital home (c).

36.   **Issue: Community property.**
Answer (d) is the correct answers. In community property states, earnings including bonuses are community property. Dividends on community property are community property. One-half of the earnings, bonus, and dividends are allocated to him; one-half to Jones.

37.   **Issue: Community property.**
Answer (b) is the correct answer. Because

community property regimes allocate one-half of the spouse's earnings during marriage, spouses can devise their entire share of the community property as they wish. Thus **all** his share of the community property (not one-half (a); not all his earnings, bonus, and dividends (c)) can be willed to the Red Cross. Jones's inheritance is her own separate property, and Smith has no elective share right in a community property jurisdiction. (d).

38. **Issue: Common law separate property.**
Answer (d) is the correct answer. Earnings, bonuses, and one's own inheritances are separate property. The other spouse has no interest in any of the items listed.

39. **Issue: Common law separate property.**
Answer (b) is the correct answer. In separate property states (with the exception of Georgia), the surviving spouse has the right to elect against the will, and receive a proportion of the deceased spouse's probate estate. All of the property in his estate including his inheritance is included to compile the surviving spouse's elective share.

40. **Issue: Common law separate property.**
Answer (d) is the correct answer. Absent fraud or undue influence, a property owner may leave all her property to whomever property owner chooses, even over the objections of family members. This can be done by will (a), or by a promise to will (b) (a contract to devise) or through a trust (c).

41. **Issue: Leasehold estate.**
Answer (c) is the correct answer. Periodic tenancies are created when the landlord and tenant agree on a starting date for the leasehold to commence, but do not fix a termination date. They continue for successive periods until one side gives notice. Because the rent is fix at a monthly rate; it is a month-to-month tenancy. Had the rental been

calculated on a yearly basis, a year-to-year tenancy would have been created. Had there been a specific termination date in the lease, the tenancy would have been a term of years (a). If the lease could be terminated at the will of each party, it would have been a tenancy at will (b) or at sufferance (d).

42. **Issue: Periodic tenancy.**
    Answer (a) is the correct answer. Each party to the lease can terminate a periodic tenancy by giving notice, usually one time period in advance. Thus, in a month-to-month, either landlord tenant can terminate by giving notice a month in advance, here on the 4th of each month. Automatic termination occurs only in a term of years at the end of the specified term (b). Only tenancies at will or at sufferance can be terminated without notice (c) and (d).

43. **Issue: Death of tenant.**
    Answer (b) is the correct answer. A leasehold is a property right. At the tenant's death, the leasehold passes to the heirs or devisees of the tenant. Thus son has inherited his father's tenancy, and may terminate it if he wishes, as may the landlord. The death of the tenant does not terminate the lease (a), nor does it constitute notice to terminate (c).

44. **Issue: Leasehold.**
    Answer (a) is the correct answer. Because both a starting and a termination date have been set a term of years has been created. That the stipulated term is less than a year does not matter. The lone issue is whether the lease specifies a fixed period. Periodic tenancies are created when the landlord and tenant agree on a starting date for the leasehold to commence, but do not fix a termination date (c). They continue for successive periods until one side gives notice. Since the leasehold cannot be terminated at will, it is not a tenancy at will (b) or at sufferance (d).

45. **Issue: Term of years.**
Answer (d) is the correct answer. Terms of years cannot be terminated prior to the expiration of the term ((a) through (c)). They expire at the termination date. Periodic tenancies allow termination with notice. At will tenancies can be terminated at will.

46. **Issue: Landlord's right to enter demised premises.**
Answer (c) is the correct answer. By leasing the premises, the landlord has passed the right to possession to the tenant. His entry without authorization in the lease, or without the consent of the tenant is a trespass, regardless of its minimal nature (d). No rights to enter are 'implied' ((a) and (b)).

47. **Issue: Leasehold.**
Answer (b) is the correct answer. Because there is not fixed term or a period mentioned, and the lease provides the right to terminate at any time a tenancy at will has been created.

48. **Issue: Tenancy at will.**
Answer (a) is the correct answer. Unlike other tenancies, the law regards the death of the tenant at will as a termination of the lease. Death ends the mutual volition that is required for a tenancy at will.

49. **Issue: Implied promises in lease.**
Answer (d) is the correct answers. Landlords promise that they have a right in the premises sufficient to create the leasehold estate (title) (a), that they have not created a conflicting estate in another (b), and that they will not interfere with the tenant's interest (quiet enjoyment) (c). Insurance is a matter for negotiation (d).

50.   **Issue: Landlord delivering actual possession.**
Answer (a) is the correct answer. The Uniform
Residential Landlord and Tenant Act reverses the
position in most American states that the landlord
conveys only a right to possession rather than
actual possession. The issue is whether the
landlord or the tenant should bear the expense of
evicting a sitting tenant. At common law, most
American jurisdictions did not place the burden on
the landlord to make certain that a third party was
wrongfully occupying the premises (b). The
exception was for short-term leases of furnished
tenancies where immediate actual possession was
implied (d).

51.   **Issue: Lease purposes no longer attainable.**
Answer (b) is the correct answer. If the purpose for
which the tenant must use the premises are stated
in the lease become no longer commercially viable,
the tenant may be able to use the premises for
other purposes under the contract law principle of
commercial frustration. Only if the articulated
purpose becomes illegal (like a brewery when
Prohibition began) could the tenant argue
impossibility (a). Since the purpose is expressed in
the lease, recourse to 'implied warranties' is not
likely. Here the use is commercial, and the
'habitability' warranty is appropriate only for
residential leaseholds (d). The implied warranty of
suitability generally relates to factors internal to the
property, like faulty heating, cooling, etc. (c).

52.   **Issue: Commercial frustration.**
Answer (b) is the correct answer. To make a case
for commercial frustration the tenant need not
prove that the landlord acted in bad faith, that he
knew that the limitation in the lease would render
the premises unprofitable (b). All he need show is
that it was not reasonably foreseeable at the time
the lease was executed that use of the tenancy as
apartment would be unprofitable. He need not

demonstrate what he knew or did know, but what he should have known as a reasonably prudent businessperson (a) (c) or (d).

53. **Issue: Commercial frustration.**
     Answer (b) is the correct answer. The least costly means would be to reform the lease to allow the tenancy to be used as commercial property. The landlord continues to get the rent reserved. Of course, the tenant may get a windfall if commercial rents are higher than residential, which seems to be the case. Rescission is a possible remedy; this would allow the landlord to find another tenant, but if the residential use is not feasible, landlord will probably only be able to get a commercial tenant (a). Landlord would probably get a windfall. The difference between the rent reserved and the fair market value of the premises as a residential apartment is probably the rent reserved if the residential purpose has been frustrated (c). The difference between the rent reserved and the fair market value of the premises as a commercial building would give tenant a windfall (d).

54. **Issue: Landlord's breach.**
     Answer (a) is the correct answer. Tenant might claim a constructive eviction. Tenant would argue that the landlord's failure to soundproof was a breach of the covenant of quiet enjoyment, that the landlord had an obligation to keep his tenants from disturbing each other. The noise level is probably not sufficient to render the premises uninhabitable (b). Suitability is used in the commercial context (d). The illegal lease remedy requires housing code violations that are probably not present here (c).

55. **Issue: Constructive eviction.**
     Answer (d) is the correct answer. For the tenant to prevail in a constructive eviction claim, tenant must prove that the landlord had an obligation to act (here quiet the neighbors), that landlord breached

that obligation, that tenant made landlord aware of the conditions (giving landlord the opportunity to cure), and that tenant moved out.

56. **Issue: Constructive eviction.**
    Answer (d) is the correct answer. The actual loss suffered by tenant is the benefit of tenant's bargain: the difference between the rent of a similar apartment without the unruly neighbors over the term of the original lease with landlord and the rent reserved. If tenant rented at a favorable rate, or rents have increased, tenant should be reimbursed for her increased costs. Expenses are speculative, and individual (a); should tenant stay at the Ritz while hunting for an alternative? Since tenant does not have to pay the landlord the rent after the constructive eviction, the landlord should not pay the entire rental cost of the alternative accommodation (b). The value of the premises to tenant is likewise speculative (c).

57. **Issue: Implied warranty of habitability.**
    Answer (b) is the correct answer. Although tenant might claim a constructive eviction, an actual eviction has not occurred; the landlord has not physically removed tenant from the premises (a). But room temperature at ninety degrees probably triggers an implied warranty of habitability claim. Suitability claims are used in the commercial context (d). The illegal lease remedy requires housing code violations at the time the lease was executed: the air conditioner worked at that point (c).

58. **Issue: Implied warranty habitability.**
    Answer (b) is the correct answer. It is only necessary for the tenant to prove that the defect is sufficiently serious to render the premises uninhabitable. The landlord need not have breached an express promise or obligation (a); all

residential leases imply habitability. The tenant
need not quit the premises to bring an action (c).

59.   **Issue: Constructive eviction.**
Answer (d) is the correct answer. Courts provide a
variety of damages for breach of the implied
warranty of habitability. Tenant could repair and
deduct (a). Or tenant could claim that tenant
should pay reduced rent, the fair rental value as is
(b); or have the rent reduced by the calculation of
the difference between the rent reserved and the
fair market value of the premises as habitable(c).
Relocation expenses are another matter (d). They
are too individualized and speculative.

60.   **Issue: Transfer.**
Answer (c) is the correct answer. Because the
transferee seems to be able to pay the rent, and
engages in the same type of commercial enterprise
as the current tenant, it seems as if the landlord is
unreasonably refusing to consent. Even though the
clause does not require the landlord's refusal to be
reasonable, the law will imply it.

61.   **Issue: Landlord's rights in sub-lease.**
Answer (c) is the correct answer. Landlord can sue
if he is in privity with the party in legal possession.
If the landlord allows tenant to assign, landlord can
sue both tenant and subtenant. Landlord is in
privity of contract with tenant, and privity of estate
with the sub-tenant. But if there is a sub-lease,
landlord can only recover against tenant (a). There
is neither privity of contract, nor privity of estate
between landlord and sub-leasee. In neither case,
can the landlord up the rent (b) and (d).

62.   **Issue: Landlord tort liability.**
Answer (d) is the correct answers. At common law,
landlord tort liability was limited to the three
contexts enumerated in the question. Some courts
have begun to extend landlord tort liability, but all

jurisdictions recognize these three exceptions to the general rule.

63. **Issue: Nuisance**

Answer (c) is the correct answers. At common law, first in time gave first in right; response (c) would have been correct. However, under the Restatement, while first in time may be a factor that is considered, it is no longer dispositive. The Restatement defines a nuisance as an intentional and unreasonable invasion by the actor of another party's interest in property.

64. **Issue: Nuisance.**

Answer (d) is the correct answer. Because the factory likely provides many jobs, and produces a product that it in demand, these factors probably outweigh the harm to a single householder (c). However, the alternative Restatement test of unreasonable conduct is appropriate in this fact situation. Here the test is whether the actor can continue to operate the business and pay compensation to the householder. The factory would need to increase the price of bricks, and if it cannot do so it ought not to be a free rider, continuing operation while requiring Jones to suffer a loss of use value of her home. The noise and dust is just the non-trespassory invasion that the Restatement contemplates (a). That the factory was first inn time is of some relevance, but is not compelling (b).

65. **Issue: Nuisance.**

Answer (b) is the correct answer. Many courts would award permanent damages in the amount of the value of the homeowner's property. This forced buy-out would allow the factory to continue to pollute, but since Jones would no longer own the house, it would not be a private nuisance to her. Awarding Jones an injunction would allow Jones to 'hold-up' the factory (a). The owner would have to pay a premium on Jones's lost value, because she could stop its entire operation. Whether she should get relocation expenses is debatable (c), but in terms of efficiency it seems unnecessary; it's an added cost, and she moved to the nuisance.

66. **Issue: Nuisance**
Answer (d) is the correct answers. Arguably the factory's good faith (b) and best efforts (c) are not an issue in nuisance law. What matters is whether the noise is a sufficient non-trespassory invasion. That they cannot operate without creating noise may go to the issue of appropriate damages (permanent damages rather than injunction).

67. **Issue: Servitudes**
Answer (b) is the correct answers. Both (a) and (c) are classic easements: interests in property held by a party that permits a party to do an affirmative act on another's property, the act which would otherwise constitute a trespass. In both cases, a vehicle owned by the holder, for example, can pass on the land of the landholder. Answer (d) is an easement in gross; the personal right to enter on to the land of another to a particular act. At common law these were know as profits. Use restrictions are best classified as equitable servitudes. or if in writing and meeting particular requirements, real covenants (b).

68. **Issue: Easements by estoppel.**
Answer (d) is the correct answer. When Smith authorized Jones to use his land for access, he created a license, authorization to use the property of another that is revocable at will by the licensor. But when Smith observed Jones making an investment in his land and in the improvement of the drive, the license became irrevocable: Smith was estopped from revoking. Easements by grant are created through the execution of a document (a). Prescriptive easements by satisfying the

requirements of adverse possession as modified to easements: open and notorious use, exclusive to others, continuous, and without the landholder's permission (b). Easements by necessity (c) arise when land is divided into two or more parcels, not the case here.

69.   **Issue: Transferability of easements.**
Answer (a) is the correct answer. When Smith sold the servient parcel (the land subject to the easement), the land still remained burdened if it was intended that the burden run with the land. Here, the type of easement suggests that the holder and the grantor would regard the interest as transferable: why else might Jones make the investment in improving the easement if it could be extinguished by sale (c). While the benefit might run with Jones's parcel, and that is less clear from the facts; easements by estoppel are frequently considered personal to the original licensee, and endure only so long as is necessary to realize the cost of the investment made in reliance (b).

70.   **Issue: Scope of easement.**
Answer (a) is the correct answer. If the parties only contemplated individual use, than Smith might be able to enjoin use; but without explicit limitations, it is likely that occasional use by guest was in the contemplation of the parties. While previous unobstructed use by the guests might be evidence of the intent of the parties, it is not necessary to prove the contemplated use (b). While easements may be personal and limited only to the individual to whom it was granted, courts would look to the circumstances; here there is not clear indication that it was so limited (d).

71.   **Issue: Termination of servitudes.**
Answer (a) is the correct answer. When the Banks acquired Jones's parcel, he owned both the dominant and servient tenement. One cannot (and

of course need not) have an easement in ones own land. Here, the holder of the servient interest also held the dominant interest. The easement was extinguished by merger. Even though Banks may have been using the drive, it was as a landowner of the drive, not as the holder of an easement. When he conveyed to Norris, he would have had to create the previous easement by granting it. This he did not do.

72. **Issue: Overuse**
Answer (c) the correct answers. Excessive use is use beyond the contemplated scope and can be enjoined. Here it is clear that the original license (which ripened into an easement) was residential rather than commercial. The easement should not be terminated unless of course the holder no longer contemplates residential use (a) and (b). There has been no merger of the dominant and servient interests (d).

73. **Issue: Implied easements.**
Answer (d) is the correct answers. Easements can be created by operation of law. When an owner of property sub-divides her property in such a way as to render the conveyed parcel landlocked, the transferee has an easement by necessity. So unity of title, severance and necessity are required. But there is no need to prove that the vendor used part of his land for the benefit of another (a quaieasment) which is required for an easement by implication.

74. **Issue: Implied easements.**
Answer (a) is the correct answer. Use restrictions in transfers are best considered equitable servitudes, unless the grant expressly directs that the property return to the grantor (b) if the condition is broken or that the grantor may re-enter (c) neither of which are specified in the restriction. Though some courts refer to such limitations as

negative easements, easements (d) are more usually affirmative interests to use the land of another.

75. **Issue: Implied easements.**
Answer (c) is the correct answer. Some courts, though not all, still require that a promise touch and concern the land. Although the term is defined differently in different jurisdictions, the general rule is that the promise must provide some economical benefit to the land. Arguably it does because fewer bars may make bars more profitable, though one may also argue that it makes a business more valuable, not the land per se. Privity (a) (b) is not a requirement to enforce the equitable servitude so long as there is notice. Promisee need not burden her own land (d). But even if no equitable servitude is found, the promise may be enforced in contract; Joe (promisee) enforces the promise against Banks (promisor).

76. **Issue: Equitable servitude.**
Answer (a) is the correct answer. Equitable servitudes were recognized by courts of equity in cases in which use restrictions could be enforced in equity against successors to the promisees's land. Since equity courts originally only allowed equitable remedies, the plaintiff could only ask for an injunction. Here Joe cannot sue Norris in contract since there was no privity of contract between them. Joe need only prove intent that the promise runs with the land and notice. Privity (c) and (d) is not necessary, though it may be used to prove notice. Mere intent to bind successors (b) is insufficient without notice of the promise to the successor of the promisor.

77. **Issue: Breach of promise.**
Answer (c) is the correct answer. Equitable servitudes were recognized by courts of equity in cases in which use restrictions that were not created in accordance with the law of real

covenants could be enforced in equity. Since equity courts originally only allowed equitable remedies, the plaintiff could only ask for an injunction. But here the restriction may meet the requirements of a real covenant.

78. **Issue: Promise Against Successors.**
Answer (a) is the correct answers. Most jurisdictions require that for a promise to bind the promisor's successors in a action for damages, the elements of a real covenant must be proved: the promise must be created by parties in horizontal privity (met here at least in some jurisdictions, since the promise was set out in a conveyance, though the early common law required mutual interests in land, and the stricter rule not met here); that the individual against whom the promise was to be enforced was in vertical privity with the promisor (met here because Norris bought from Banks); that the promise touches and concerns the land (defined differently in different jurisdictions, but requiring some benefit to inure to the land, questionable here); and that the parties intended the promise to run with the land (bind successors). Here there is no language in the covenant expressly binding future holders (and her heirs and assigns) (a); nor is likely that the court (though some do) will find the covenant not to compete to sufficiently benefit Joe's land as opposed to his business (c). They are not always personal (b), that is enforceable only against the promisor.. If the court did find intent that the covenant to compete binds successors, and sufficient touch and concern, it would enforce it against successors not just against the promisor (d), so long as Joe and Banks are in privity, and Banks and Norris are in privity, both the horizontal and vertical privity requirements are met.

79. **Issue: Enforcement by successor to promisor.**
Answer (b) is the correct answer. The successor in

interest of the promisee can sue to enforce the promise as against successors so long as it was intended that successors to the parcel benefited should also have the benefit of the promise. So if the requirements of an equitable servitude are met, (probably) Moe can sue for an injunction. The real covenant is more doubtful because intent and touch and concern may be lacking. But if were found Moe could also sue for damages.

80. **Issue: Public Use Requirement.**
Answer (d) is the correct answer. The Supreme Court of the United States (as opposed to some State Supreme Courts) defers to the legislative judgment as to the appropriate circumstances in which the takings power can be exercised under the "public use" requirement of the Fifth Amendment to the United States Constitution. So long as there is no bad faith in selecting the property to be taken, the legislature has wide latitude in determining what is a public use.

81. **Issue: Just Compensation.**
Answer (c) is the correct answers. Just compensation required by the Fifth Amendment is the fair market value (what a willing buyer would pay a willing seller) of the property and its fixtures. Since the government did not acquire the lost profits, or indeed profit from the move, it will not reimburse these costs. All of the other choices relate to the intrinsic value of the land.

82. **Issue: Division of award for leased premises.**
Answer (c) is the correct answer. Under the "undivided fee rule", both interests are compensated. First the value of premises and fixtures is calculated. Then the value of the lease is calculated (difference between the fair rental value of the lease less the rent reserved for the term), and allocated to the tenant. The landlord receives the remaining value.

83.   **Issue: Just compensation.**
Answer (c) is the correct answer. The Supreme
Court has held that a permanent physical
occupation of private land pursuant to government
regulation triggers compensation even if the
occupation is minimal. The degree of interference
goes to the issue of the amount of compensation
not the need for it. Just compensation is not
required where there is an average reciprocity of
advantage (a), because the landowner receives some
tangible benefit for the loss occasioned by the
regulation. In some situations, when the
government exacts a concession there may be the
need for compensation ("the unconstitutional
condition"), but not where the ban on development
would be justified (b). Mere decrease in value is
insufficient to always trigger compensation (d).

84.   **Issue: Regulatory Taking.**
Answer (b) is the correct answer. In <u>Lucas</u>, the
Supreme Court held that when a government
regulation renders land valueless, the state's
prohibition must be calculated to prevent a use
that would have been a nuisance at common law.
If it did so act, it would not take away any
development right, but merely preclude that which
a landowner could not do, create a nuisance. So if
the court was willing to regard the prohibition to
divide as not preventing a common law nuisance,
the court might regard the value of the hoped for
second lot as valueless. There is no physical
occupation (d), nor has a short moratorium been
considered a taking (c). Since he did not intend to
sub-divide at purchase, no investment-backed
expectation has been thwarted (a).

85.   **Issue: Regulatory taking.**
Answer (a) is the correct answer. Government may
only condition the granting of a permit upon some
dedication of property if there is a close nexus
between the loss to the public occasioned by the

development and the dedication. Here the division permits a second house, and a second house does not have an appreciable affect on public access to the beach. If somehow it made access more difficult the nexus would be satisfied. So the dedication required in the question might well be regarded as an unconstitutional condition. Because what has been required is the dedication of an easement and the easement is always there, there is a permanent cast to the exaction. But the public is not in permanent possession of his land (c). His property is still valuable, and the use contemplated at purchase has not been forbidden (b). The strip still has value (d); he can use it.

86. **Issue: Time, Place And Manner Restrictions.**
Answer (a) is the correct answer. Even though the access right does make his land modestly less valuable (d) and the gate offers no average reciprocity of advantage because it does not benefit his land (b), the fact that he can control access gives him the type of time, place, and manner controls that militate against finding the occupation a permanent one. He can regulate the use of the easement.

87. **Issue: <u>Euclid</u> rule.**
Answer (b) is the correct answer. <u>Euclid</u> did not consider whether as applied the zoning plan adopted by the Village was or was not a taking (a) and (d). Nor did it expressly rule on whether the zoning board's plan may trigger compensation if it devalued land held by private owners (c). It held that zoning was a valid exercise or the police power, and therefore its use was not per se a taking.

88. **Issue: Amortization Of Non-Conforming Uses.**
Answer (d) is the correct answers. In fact, zoning boards are given wide latitude in allowing pre-existing uses to continue as non-conforming uses after a change in zoning. The zoning board can

make individualized decisions based on any of the factors so long as their judgments are reasonable and rational. But how far the store is to another store does not necessarily impact the zoned property (d).

89. **Issue: Time, place and manner restrictions.**
Answer (d) is the correct answer. Although protected expression, the speaker and/or performer rights may be limited. Zoning regulations that permit limit venues where expression can be exercised are subject to intermediate scrutiny. Instead of requiring the government to show that the regulation was the least restrictive means of limiting exercise (strict scrutiny) (b) or a rational basis (the a reasonable legislature could find that the regulation is necessary to protect a public interest) (c), the court requires some evidence that the regulation is targeted towards a particular permissible end, and is not gauged to impede expression because the content is objectionable.

90. **Issue: Exclusionary Zoning.**
Answer (b) is the correct answer. The Supreme Court has allowed municipalities to determine what constitutes a family for the purposes of single family zoning ordinances. The one exception is that multigenerational families must be considered as a single family. Answers (a), (c), and (d) pass the rational basis test.

91. **Issue: Exclusionary zoning.**
Answer (d) is the correct answer. The Supreme Court has not held such practices unconstitutional (a). The Fair Housing Act does not address that issue either (b). Led by the New Jersey Supreme Court in the <u>Mount Laurel</u> case, a few courts, but certainly not most (c), have found the right to affordable housing protected by state constitutions.

92.   **Issue: Exclusionary zoning.**
Answer (b) is the correct answer. The landowner
must show that the granting of the ordinance would
not thwart the comprehensive plans aims (a), and
the welfare of the community will not be
jeopardized. Both unique hardship (b) and
unnecessary hardship (d) must be shown. But to
show unique hardship the landowner need not
show he is the only one adversely effected, just that
the hardship is not generalized, that it does not
affect most or all of the other properties in question.

93.   **Issue: Statute of Frauds.**
Answer (a) is the correct answer. In order for an
agreement for the sale of land to be enforced, the
Statute of Frauds requires that it be in writing and
signed by the party against whom it is to be
enforced. Usually it is the sales contract that
satisfies the Statute, but a less formal instrument
setting out the parties, the property, and the price
satisfies the Statute so long as it is signed (b). A
deposit is not a necessary requirement (c). Smith
has not satisfied the "part performance" exception
(d); he has not paid the price, entered or improved
the property.

94.   **Issue: Statute of Frauds.**
Answer (c) is the correct answer. Had Jones cashed
the check, the terms on the reverse substantially
satisfy the parties, the property, and the price
requirement of the Statute; and had he cashed the
check assent to the terms might have been implied.
The need for a signature would be waived. But he
did not so there is no acceptance of the terms ((a)
and (d)). Receipt of the check (b) is not enough.

95.   **Issue: Statute of Frauds.**
Answer (a) is the correct answers. Cashing the
check might have been considered acceptance of
Smith's offer. Likewise, had Smith entered the land
without Jones's objection, there would have been

sufficient part performance on his part to come with in the exception of Statute. Neither full payment (b) nor the building contract (c) would be sufficient. Had the builder entered with permission (and not without) there would have been acceptance.

96. **Issue: Statute of Frauds.**
     Answer (b) is the correct answer. Here there is an oral promise and reliance; equitable estoppel applies - the writing requirement is waived. Wholly gratuitous promises are not enforceable (a), the price term though not definite is sufficiently ascertainable to be enforced (c), and there seems to be a public policy interest rather than objection (d) to recognizing the contract.

97. **Issue: Marketable Title.**
     Answer (a) is the correct answer. Undisclosed restrictions on land render title unmarketable. The single-family dwelling restriction in the title, if undisclosed, renders title unmarketable (b). Although the agreement was to purchase residential land, "single family only" is a different restrictions, and a narrower one. The existence of residential restrictions (a) is consistent with the contract; zoning does not render title unmarketable, because buyer can enquire (c); and title is still marketable even if the structures are not in conformity to law (d). Marketability issues deal with land restrictions, not with fixtures. The buyer should have examined the building.

98. **Issue: Marketable title.**
     Answer (a) is the correct answer. The misdescription in a title deed in the chain of title renders title unmarketable. Each of the other choices does not render title unmarketable. Only a guardian need execute the deed in the name of the minor titleholder (b); so long as the will has been probated or an administration undertaken, an heir

or legatee may transfer marketable title (c), as may a corporate titleholder where the appropriate officer has executed the deed.

99.   **Issue: Risk of loss.**
Answer (a) is the correct answer. Most jurisdictions recognize the doctrine of equitable conversion: the buyer (not the seller) (d) is deemed owner, and risk of loss passes to the buyer. The particular dangerous nature of the property is not relevant (b) and (c). If Smith had misrepresented, there might be some action for fraud, but it would not affect the outcome of action for specific performance.

100.   **Issue: Risk of loss.**
Answer (a) is the correct answer. Equitable conversion will not be implemented if the parties agree to allocation of risk. Here they did. Whether there was insurance or not and which party held it should not be relevant. All that could be insured was the interest that the parties held in law. That Smith had it (b) doesn't change the doctrine's outcome; not did Jones's belief about the when she needed insurance cover (c) and (d) relevant.